Communities of Hope

D1100098

Communities of Hope

A Lent Course

Edited by

R U S S E L L   B O W M A N - E A D I E
and
G R A H A M   D O D D S

with contributions from

Robin Eames
Jean Vanier
Kathy Galloway
Jim Thompson
Dame Cicely Saunders

Illustrations by Sarah John

DARTON · LONGMAN + TODD

First published in 1998 by
Darton, Longman and Todd Ltd
1 Spencer Court
140–142 Wandsworth High Street
London SW18 4JJ

ISBN 0–232–52262–6

A catalogue record for this book is available from the British
Library.

Illustrations by Sarah John
Designed by Sandie Boccacci
Phototypeset in 9.75/12.5 pt Monotype Times by Intype London Ltd
Printed and bound in Great Britain by
Redwood Books, Trowbridge, Wiltshire

Contents

Acknowledgements

The editors and publisher are grateful to David Adam for permission to use the prayer 'Desert Waters' from *Tides and Seasons* published by Triangle books and to Alain Boublil Music Limited for lyrics from 'I Dreamed a Dream' from *Les Miserables*, a musical by Alain Boublil and Claude-Michel Schönberg, lyrics by Herbert Kretzmer, Alain Boublil and Jean-Mark Natel. Thanks are due to the Revd Jeremy T. Law, Lazenby Chaplain of the University of Exeter, for his early theological consultancy work with the editors. We are also grateful to the Revd Alan Nicholls who read and corrected the script.

Introduction

In the long-running and popular musical *Les Miserables*, the character Fantine sings 'I dreamed a dream' as in despair she recalls happier days before her dreams turned sour:

> I dreamed a dream in time gone by
> when hope was high
> and life worth living.
> I dreamed that love would never die.
> I dreamed that God would be forgiving.
>
> I had a dream my life would be
> so different from this hell I'm living,
> so different now from what it seemed.
> Now life has killed
> the dream I dreamed.

Many people's experience of life is that it kills dreams. Whilst they may not go on necessarily to describe it as a living hell, it does none the less feel as though dreams get shattered and broken; and sometimes we find ourselves picking up the pieces.

The Christian story has always recognised that this is a precondition of our living and yet it has refused to accept that this is the last word. The church community came into existence through the experience of brokenness and pain and anxiety about the future. Always though, it expressed the single conviction that hope is born from its Easter joy, that Christ is alive and that 'nothing in all creation', as Paul says, 'can separate us from the love of God in Christ'.

In fact, in spite of the odds, we seem to be made for hope. It is a very important part of our being so we talk about our personal hopes for our ambitions and for our world. We even use the phrase 'hoping against hope' which in a powerful way speaks into the pain of any situation. Few would doubt that hope has to find itself in any pattern of human life. However, the Christian hope does not just rest in the resurrection itself but is bound up in a way of loving, caring and forgiving.

This Lent Course is based on the view that each Christian community needs to become more the kind of community which is attractive to people because the reality of pain and brokenness is always in the process of being transformed through the mysterious, transfiguring love of God. That is hope. So often this is lost sight of as churches struggle with survival or as they have got locked into routines and patterns which in themselves are destructive or deadening. Each of our contributors in different ways has had the experience of community development and ministry. So the question that we put to them was, 'What can we learn from other kinds of communities which can enable churches, whether small or large, to become places that truly reflect the caring, healing, forgiving love of God?' In that sense they are *communities of hope*.

We would like to thank all the contributors to this Lent Course. They gave us more than we have used in the text of the book, through the sharing of some of their own personal story with us and this was both a privilege and a joy. Each one has been an inspiration to us in our own journey.

Accompanying this book is a cassette tape which contains extracts from the interviews we held with each contributor. The tape is designed to be used in conjunction with the book and will help guide groups through each session. It is suggested that each group member has a copy of the book. Only one cassette per group is needed.

Russell Bowman-Eadie
Graham Dodds

Session 1

A Segment of Eternity

Becoming communities of reconciliation in
the midst of conflict and division

with Robin Eames

Flying into Belfast City airport gives the traveller a wonderful view of just how beautiful Northern Ireland is. The green land, punctuated by lakes, glistens as you descend. As we drove out of the airport we wondered what Northern Ireland would really be like. So much has been portrayed of this area as 'troubled'. The contrast between such beauty and the portrayal of a 'troubled' country was strangely mysterious. Like Jesus in Gethsemane, who also was 'troubled', we sought to find out how hope might be forged in adversity. As Jesus struggled with his future, so these communities are also engaged in the often painful journey to find and achieve hope. One man, who amongst others, has been at the forefront of Northern Ireland's search for hope, is Archbishop Robin Eames. Because of his experience and understanding of some of the most troubled places and situations in the world we interviewed him to find out from where he sees faith and hope springing.

Preparing to meet an archbishop, even if you are a clergyman, is quite daunting. We'd heard a great deal of Archbishop Eames and seen him on the television but thinking of meeting him face to face made us slightly nervous. We didn't need to be. The gospel writers sometimes remark on Jesus 'looking with compassion' on the people. We imagine they saw that mostly in his eyes and likewise Robin Eames' eyes burn with care for his people. His sharp mind is locked into an intense pastoral concern. Charming, fatherlike and charged with God's purpose, he impressed us both as we talked.

The Archbishop brings to his work a love which is forged from faith, study and experience. He speaks about his faith not in a distant, stuffy, academic way but rather in resonance with his listener – he's empathic, and also learned. His opinions are plucked from a wealth and depth of theological study. His experience made us gasp at times when we heard of his courage and humility in his ministry. It's true that he has been intimately involved in some of the events that have shaped the world, both in the country where he lives and abroad over the past years. Yet there was no blowing of his own trumpet. Rather, the music of his voice is gentle, challenging, calling, moving and profound.

Augustine of Hippo is reputed to have said to his congregation, 'For you, I am a bishop, with you, I am a Christian', adding that the latter was a lot safer and less demanding than the former. Robin Eames shines as a Christian and spends himself as a bishop. Formidable problems have faced him through his ministry and it's obvious that he has been given courage as his faith has been tested. Yet he owns, as his own responsibility, the will to take the message that has become his life and to go where God has sent him.

So as we sat in one of his meeting rooms in Church House, Armagh, we asked him how he would define hope:

> I always think of hope as basically a personal thing. I see hope basically in terms of people's aspirations for the future rather than looking over their shoulder. When you take that into a Christian context of course, you are talking about what lies ahead of you in life, what lies ahead of you in your hopes for the future, what lies ahead of you in your vision of what the future may be. Whether it is at a personal level in your home life, in your

4

parish life, in your work life, in the purely Christian sense I tie it down totally to my conviction of life after death and that's what people can look forward to.

I think particularly of the time when, on behalf of the Archbishop of Canterbury, I was involved in the attempts to get the release of the hostages in Lebanon. We were doing various things and working, we thought, at that time in total secrecy, getting various things in place. I remember so well, when the Irish hostage Brian Keenan was released, spending twenty-four hours with him in his hospital as he returned to Dublin. He sat cross-legged on his bed in a pair of running shorts, because he couldn't bear to have bedclothes put over any part of his body after three or four years in total isolation and captivity. Instinctively I asked him, 'What kept you going?' He said, 'I kept going as long as I had hope. The minute they managed to destroy hope for me I began to go downhill. Once hope was restored, from listening to the BBC Overseas Broadcasts, I immediately began to see hope again.'

Now I use that as an example for the Christian definition of hope. I believe hope, for the ordinary man and woman in the pew, is a hope that is based entirely on mere knowledge and expectation of what God is offering to them in their own life. For their family they hope for the wellbeing of their son and their daughter. They hope that the job position will improve, they hope that their own financial situation will improve. Hope in the Christian sense is an extension of that because hope is based on what we see and know and what we believe will happen.

We look back over our shoulder and learn from the experience of what life has taught us and on that we base our hope for the future, not just biblically, not just in Scripture, but on the knowledge that the God who has brought us so far is not going to leave us at this moment. We shall be embraced by those arms and by that certainty.

Secondly, I think Christian hope is the hope that what we are experiencing in life is but a segment of eternity. While we are privileged, either in ministry or in lay discipleship or even in ordinary everyday life, to glimpse just a part of the jigsaw, hope and certainty form a barometer of our faith. Our faith will be a future mirror-reflection of what our hope is at this moment.

I think of pastoral experiences in the situations where I have ministered for years in violence and in sudden death and in destruction and in misery. So many people have absolutely amazed me by the way in which they have clung to hope. The very people you would expect to have absolutely no confidence for the future because of what evil and violence has done to them are the people who have taught me a lesson. They are the people who have said, 'Look, it can't go on like this. Life will not go on like this.' Our faith is teaching us that in the future God will be there, as he has brought us to this point, and as he has been standing beside us through this misery and this loss.

The third thing I say about hope is that it is contained in the figure, the ministry and the image of Christ. Christ-like hope means that life, as it is, is but a momentary pause in the span of eternity. The Christian has always managed to base his hope

for the future on the knowledge that God tran-
scends the instantaneous reaction, the instantaneous experience and places that in the whole
spectrum of what our life will be.

And the last thing I would say about my definition of Christian hope is that I have always felt
it is based on the simple lesson that in the end
goodness is far greater than badness, than a lack
of hope, than frustration, than the power that
comes when we are frustrated. I have seen in my
own experience working in Northern Ireland time
and time again, examples of people whose faith
may have been a very simple, workaday faith
moving from incident to incident, experience to
experience, who are saying, 'You know my faith is
seeing me through . . .', 'Don't worry about me . . .',
'My faith will get me through this . . .', 'My faith
is deep enough to tell me that God won't neglect
me in the days that come, no matter what happens'.
There is nothing in this world or in the world to
come that can ever separate us from the love of
God in Christ. When we know that from the experience of the past, it gives us the basis for the hope
for the future.

So hope is based on looking ahead, seeing life as a
segment of eternity, recognising God's ability to see
the overall plan. It's created by knowing that there is
nothing greater than the love of God. How then can
this become a reality? What's the cash value of such
thinking? In particular we asked the Archbishop to say
by what means he sees society reaching for this hope,
how the individual Christian and indeed the Church
can help it come about.

In the political sense, we are given great promises by a new government that this is what they are going to do, to be a more compassionate, a more caring society. In terms of society itself, so much is being spent on trying to give people a better life-style, a better hope: the elderly, the sick, and the hospital services and so on.

In a sense, I think society, which is largely secularised in my opinion, is writing a new agenda of what values it thinks are important. We like to think we are a communal society, we like to think we are a caring society but when it comes down to actual cases there are many many people who say to me today, 'My greatest feeling at the moment is that I don't count as an individual. I'm a number on someone's list, I'm a number on a computer, I'm simply a reference point to the Inland Revenue or to the doctor, or to the dentist' – or to whoever it is.

I believe hope from ministry is to say to people, 'Look, you do matter as an individual, you do count as a person.' That represents the shift that I am trying to describe because the Christian hope is not dependent on the sort of things that society so often bases its agenda for the future on. The Christian hope is to say, 'Look, as you are, with all the warts and with all the nice things, and with the smiles as well as the frowns, you do matter to God, you do matter to a God who cares for you. You may lose sight of that presence, you may be totally immune to that presence because of what you are going through, but the hope that we can offer in pastoral ministry is you do count.'

The hope that we are bringing in a Christian

sense to a secularised society is: 'In many cases you are basing your value judgement on things that will be transient, things that will pass, things that perhaps will be of a different value judgement this time tomorrow. However, there are certain basic hopes, there are certain basic aspirations which *cannot* be watered down simply because of what society may be seeing or doing. The basis for Christian hope is that the things of the moment have got to be viewed in terms of eternity, in terms of our entire lifestyle, in terms of what happens to us as individuals.

I have to be honest and say that what worries me about all this is what many young people say to me, 'We haven't lost faith in God, we haven't lost faith in spiritual values but we don't see that God and we don't see those values in your pulpit or your sanctuary. We don't see that element of hope. We are too conditioned now by the sort of agendas which society is giving us and we are longing for a spiritual dimension to hope but we are not finding it in society. We are looking for it in the Church, but we don't always find it there.' To me that is a very sobering question for the whole concept of ministry.

Lent is a time to consider questions soberly and seriously. It is also often perceived to be a time to give things up, though today we might speak more about taking things up than giving things up. For example, consider a discipline of daily prayer or a period of study each day. These things are easy to enthuse about but often difficult to put into practice and even harder to continue. We'd like to take positive steps to encourage our faith and prayer but it's so hard. Many of us have such crowded diaries or busy ways of living that we can almost push God and hope out.

It seems it's a matter of who's in control of ourselves. On the one hand we have our own agendas; we like to tell God the answer before we ask him the question. On the other hand we want God to be God. We asked the Archbishop why we have our own agendas.

I have a feeling that there is a simple answer to that – from my experience, we're so confident that we know better than anyone else. That's a great spiritual fault. I have to guard against that, I'll be honest with you. I have to guard against that every day I live. I know exactly what I have put in my diary when my secretary says: 'At 10 o'clock you are doing this, at 11 o'clock you are doing that and you are free at 1 o'clock to get something to eat.' I've a fair notion what's going to happen to me on any one day and I'll do what preparation I can but I also have to say, as I say my prayers in the morning, 'O God, fill in the gaps. Be the God not just of 10 o'clock but in the gap between 10 and 10.30 and 11 because I don't know what is going to happen then.'

And in my ministry, again getting back to my situation, all my colleagues in the ministry know that you can throw the diary out of the window because the phone call will come and you will be plunged into a pastoral situation of caring which is going to take every ounce of your spirituality. The only way that I can face a day like that, even when we are removed from the atrocities and in the peace process, the only way I can deal with that as

10

a Christian, is simply to say, 'God, you know better than I do. In God's Name help me to fill those gaps and tell me what to say and what to do.'

I once met a man, I won't give his name, but I once met a leading trade unionist whose name was a household word throughout the United Kingdom. When I got to know him, I don't think I would have given an ounce for his church membership or tradition, I never looked on him as a church person. I was to learn better. He may not have been in a pew every Sunday but he had a depth of faith that shamed me because I remember him saying he always had a daily practice – he went into his office in the headquarters of his Union in London in the morning. It never varied. He shut the door and he locked it. He took the phone off the hook. He closed the window. He shut the diary. He put his hands in front of him on the desk and he said: 'O God, I know roughly what I am doing today. You know better. Help me to know what to do and to say when words fail me.' I've always remembered that and I think that is one of the greatest spiritual lessons a non-churchgoer has ever shared with me as I tried to do my faith pilgrimage.

Words often fail us when facing a crisis like a young mother dying of cancer or a child run over but in the face of the persistent horrors and atrocities in Northern Ireland that the Archbishop referred to it must be tempting to lose faith in God or at least to find it hard to make sense of his ways. We asked the Archbishop to reflect on how to keep going in such circumstances, not only in the wider conflicts but also in the intimate pastoral problems of everyday life.

I tend to find that my thinking is very much couched in the instantaneous situation. I feel it is of great importance to be able to bring one's faith into a situation, not as you would like it to be but as it really is. So first of all I have to really understand what the exact situation is. It's no use talking to a couple whose marriage is on the rocks about the great principles of the happy home. They've had their happy home and it's not happy any more and they say, 'Thank you very much for your spiritual guidance but it has absolutely nothing to do with what we are feeling.' If, as I have so often, I sit through the long hours of the night with someone who is battling against alcoholism, it's no use saying to them, 'Incidentally this is doing you a terrible amount of harm, you are ruining your liver, you are ruining everything', when they are dying to get rid of me to get on to the next drink. What I have to do is to understand completely what their situation is.

Now there are human barriers to that. We never disclose *everything* that we feel or know to our greatest friend, our wife, or our closest – we don't do that, we are human beings with protective shields. What I have to do in a purely pastoral sense is to get alongside that person, to try and put myself as close as I can to where they *are* and to understand what brought them to that point and what *may* be the hope that will take them into better pastures, a better roadway. That's why when I talked about hope I talked about hope being based not just on what you thought would happen but on what had brought you to that point in terms of experience.

I use this little phrase, 'the theology of the instantaneous'. It sounds terribly important, doesn't it? What it really means to me is that I like to go into a situation and then try and apply my theology to it. Surely Christians have to **listen** before they speak, to **pray** before they listen and to **experience** before they even start the process.

I went to Uganda with my wife and we spent some days in the refugee camps and we talked through a translator to the widows of the Sudanese civil war which was happening at that time. I remember so well, the sort of question in my mind was how you explain the situation to the teeming thousands of refugees that there's a God who cares for them, when all they want is a glass of water, when the woman has the baby in her arms and her breasts will no longer feed it. I picked up a little girl called Christine – we were doing a TV programme on a visit to the camps for Independent Television – and I nursed this little girl and talked to the camera. Oh, I was presumptuous, I knew all the answers . . . look listeners . . . look viewers . . . look at all this misery . . . what are you going to do about it back in Britain? And then the producer held up his hand, he said, 'I think we should move on.' I said, 'Why?' He said, 'The child in your arms is dead.'

That is the situation in which you question your faith. That's the situation in which you talk about Aids, you talk about leprosy and you talk about cancer, and you talk about the things that pose questions that are very difficult to give a consistent realistic answer to from our presumptuous pastoral ministry. I think one of the greatest things the Christian can learn is the lesson of what to do when you haven't got the pat answer, when you haven't got the bland phrase. It's then I go to my phrase, 'When they forget that you weren't able to frame the word, they'll remember you were there.' The Christ that I believe in is the same Christ who walks beside the person and says, 'I am with you because I have been through it myself. I know what temptation is like, I know what human suffering is like, I know what disappointment is like and I know what bereavement is like. But I want to walk beside you and tell you not even that can separate you from my love.'

It's interesting to note that Jesus didn't tell his disciples what kept him going when the going was tough. Yet he had hard questions to answer, a physically punishing schedule and sometimes troubles that made him sweat blood. Archbishop Eames, like all leaders in the Church, has faced some very difficult decisions in his ministry. Far from shirking these or compromising his faith he acts out of conviction and commitment. Although he was reluctant to talk about himself, we persuaded him to tell us what keeps him going, what keeps this conviction live within him.

Well, I think in all honesty I have to be almost parsonical in my answer and that is to turn back to my faith that I have talked about. It's a very personal thing to me. It's a faith which in a personal sense I don't often talk about except in chats such

14

as we are having. But could I give you an example of what I think I am trying to say to you?

Out of the blue some years ago when Northern Ireland was engulfed in horrendous violence, mediators came to me and said would I meet the terrorists, and I had to have a long agonising thought – was it right for someone in my position to talk to those who were killing and murdering and torturing and blowing places up. To cut a long story short, I went back to my personal revelation of what the gospel was and I said Christ wouldn't turn a blind eye to this if there was a chance of trying to find peace, so yes, I agreed to see them. We had three or four meetings, as is now well documented, and to cut a long story short, at the end of it came the ceasefire. I don't say that my input was the only input but they tell me in things they are now saying that it had an impression.

Now what did I say to them? I listened to them. I asked them to justify what they were doing in their terms and then I started to talk to them about the gospel of Christ. Not the gospel of Christ that's for the goody-goodies who go to church every Sunday and who eat their polo mints during the sermon! That's not the gospel that I tried to talk to them about. I talked to them about their import-ance as individuals, that most of them had once been baptised. I talked to them about the God of judgement and the God of compassion and I talked about the advantages of peace for all of us.

One of them said something to me which I will never forget as long as I live, he said, 'You have triggered a memory in my mind that I had long forgotten.' He said, 'I have killed people myself with my own bare hands, I have escaped justice and I have planned atrocities. One day, long ago, I was a Sunday School pupil in a small church and something I was taught then has haunted me in what I am now doing in my adult life.' It was simply this: 'What will you answer, son?' the teacher said, looking at him, 'What will your answer be, son, when God says to you, "What have you done with your life?"' I relate that to the question, 'What keeps me going?' The knowledge that one day I am going to have to answer the question: 'What have I done with my opportunities?'

Is sleeping in, in the morning, losing an opportunity to do something more that you could be doing if you were out there doing it? I'm a hands-on sort of person. I don't necessarily like others to have to do what I'm not prepared to do. If someone's got to get their hands dirty, I'd better get mine dirty first. If I ask clergy to deal with a horrendous social problem, I can't honestly convince them they ought to do it unless I know something about what I'm talking about. It is in the battle of faith for me that unless I have tried to experience some of the things that I believe God wants others to listen to and to think about, unless I have experienced something of that, I feel like a hypocrite, I feel my words are empty.

The second thing that keeps me going is the love of those close to me, who understand and support me, who understand all my failings, understand all my weakness and say, 'Come on, think again, that's not true what you're saying.'

Thirdly, and this is the one that perhaps makes most sense to me, I believe every single human life has a purpose. I don't care who it is, I don't care what their situation, I believe God has a purpose for every single life and when I walk down Piccadilly and see the people bedding down for the night behind the cardboard boxes, when I go into the House of Lords and hear the great and the good debating issues of national importance, when I stand beside the bed of someone dying of heart disease or cancer, or when I am given the gift of a little child to baptise and it looks at me and coos up and grabs hold of my stole and pulls at it, and I say, 'I wonder what the future has for this child'. I reflect on it at Confirmation when I say, 'I have no crystal ball. I don't know what lies ahead of you in life but I do know this, the God who has brought you to this place is the God who is not going to neglect you now.'

As we left Belfast, we came away with some of the Archbishop's conviction about hope. All communities need leaders and, as Augustine implied, it is risky to lead the Church, it takes particular people. The sacrifice that our leaders make may never be known to any but God, yet if their hope fails what is there for the rest of us? The key to great leadership in Archbishop Eames' ministry is to keep hope alive by prayer, study, listening, pastoral care, reflection and humility, all based on experience. This will not be achieved by hiding in a manse or housegroup but rather by getting out of church into everyday life and living Christianity, getting dirty hands, finding courage to face fear and above all allowing God to be God.

Suggestions for Further Reading

Ann Morisy, *Beyond the Good Samaritan* (Mowbray, 1997)

Brian Keenan, *An Evil Cradling* (Hutchinson, 1992)

GROUP WORK

Reminder: These are suggested questions. Please feel free to be selective, adapt them or make up some of your own.

1. 'We like to think we are a communal society . . . but when it comes down to actual cases there are many many people who say to me today, "My greatest feeling . . . is that I don't count as an individual"' (p. 8). What does it mean to count as an individual? What changes in your church would help it to become more of a community? How could you set about putting them into practice?

2. In what ways could your church congregation be said either to collude with or to adapt to the values of society? How does the gospel challenge these?

3. How much has your church grown or declined over the last few years? What do you think the causes are? How are people invited to become part of the congregation?

4. Jot down some of the things that would help you grow spiritually. Are there things that your church could do to help you grow more in your life of prayer?

5. Archbishop Eames speaks of the practice of a non church-going trade unionist who sets aside a time of prayer. What spirituality have some other non

church-going people taught you? Why do you think they have not made connections with the church?

6. What do you feel are some of the 'basic aspirations' in the Christian faith to which Archbishop Eames was referring on page 9? Why can't they be 'watered down'? How do you see some of them being diluted?

7. 'When they forget that you weren't able to frame the word, they'll remember you were there' (p. 14). Archbishop Eames believes we need to learn that we haven't got pat answers – but we can empathise. Give examples of how this has worked out for you in practice. Why is it sometimes difficult to listen?

8. We are reminded of the troubles in Northern Ireland – for many years a place of tension, conflict and terrible acts of violence. In community life there will be conflict. How do you handle conflict in your congregation? What sorts of things do members fight about? What happens if there's no resolution?

9. Read again the Archbishop's meeting with terrorists (pp. 15–16). In what sense could it be said that he was proclaiming the gospel? Are there important lessons we need to learn from this experience like 'Love your enemies', 'Do good to those who wish to hate you'?

Encountering Scripture

Archbishop Eames says, when speaking about his visit to Uganda, 'How do you explain the situation to the teeming thousands of refugees that there's a God who cares for them, when all they want is a glass of water?' (p. 13)

Is the main reason for giving to aid programmes a need to satisfy our own conscience or a genuine desire to help eliminate the inequalities which produce such injustices and human suffering?

Read what St Paul says in his appeal to the church in Corinth of how poor people can be inspired to help one another (2 Corinthians 8:1–5).

Macedonia is what we might call an urban priority area. It once had many resources like minerals, timber and a salt trade. Under Roman occupation it had declined. People had become very poor, but the Macedonian Christians actually begged to be allowed to be generous. Money is no substitute for love but it is a very real expression of our love. There is a phrase we sometime use, 'It's the poor that helps the poor'. What does this passage say to us who are by this world's standards rich?

How realistic are we when it comes to our financial planning in the church? How far could it be said to reflect the priorities of the gospel?

You may like to use this prayer at the end of your discussion. First spend a few moments reflecting quietly on what you have been talking about and helping each other discover.

Lord, for ourselves and all people we pray for
   peace.
Help us to feel its power, its promise and its hope.
Give to each one of us the courage to stand by
   what we know to be true
and just
and honest
and pure
and lovely.
Help us always to be ready to praise you

20

and through our praise to practise all that does
justice to your holiness.
So may we truly reflect the image of divine love
and rejoice in the marvellous gifts which you have
given us
and which are hallowed by your name,
through Jesus Christ our Lord. Amen.

Session 2

Home for the Homeless

Becoming communities of welcome for those who feel marginalised in life

with Jean Vanier

It seems almost trite to say that we live in an age of great uncertainty. What age has not experienced times of real hardship and anxiety? Yet today, partly because of better communications, we have become perhaps even more aware of the fact that the world itself is in some kind of crisis. In spite of all the great advances that have been made in every avenue of science and learning we know that poverty, hunger, unemployment and homelessness are on the increase. Factors affect our global economy which could mean that future generations will be less financially secure. The future, rather than holding out some kind of promise, might appear to be more of a threat. If the world is troubled then we should expect the Church to be troubled, at least in the sense that it too is experiencing times of instability and change. Indeed so worrying is it that some congregations appear to have lost even the imagination to think that God is calling them to a future that is filled with hope.

We have in the process become suspicious of packaged programmes and quick-fix answers which hardly touch the root of the problem. They seem only to provide some kind of temporary relief. The fact is that the Church has nearly always had to struggle with understanding its own identity because it has no definitive blueprint. Even the New Testament provides us with no one model of 'church' but rather with a picture of emerging communities which are diverse and sometimes contradictory and deeply influenced by the surrounding culture.

For example, the first letter of Peter appears to have been addressed to aliens and strangers. That is, although they were Christian converts they none the less, for one reason or another, did not belong to the wider society (1 Peter 1:1–2). Their experience was of not belonging, of being what we would call today marginalised, which of course meant that they were more often than not the scapegoats for whatever economic or social tensions were around. It was to these people that Peter writes words about having a whole new identity through faith in Jesus Christ, and in so doing he paints a portrait of a church that could best be described as a real home for the homeless (1 Peter 1:3–2:10). Those who belonged to these communities actually experienced loving acceptance.

We do not need to look very far for those we would call 'homeless' in our own society – adults and children who have been either physically, emotionally or sexually abused, the divorced, the chronically addicted, people who suffer any kind of disability or handicap and, as is so often the case, the families who suffer with them. The question for us is, 'What happens when the Christian community becomes a place where people are accepted for who they are, which then releases all the potential for what they might also become?'

To help us in this exploration we approached Jean Vanier. It was in 1964 that he founded the first L'Arche community in France. Since then both L'Arche communities and the Faith and Light communities have sprung up in many other countries. They are built upon the single conviction that communities should be places of joy and celebration for those who in the community at large have little or nothing to celebrate because they feel alienated through disability. Of course the traditional response to people with mental handicaps has been to marginalise them even more by institutionalising them, often in our oldest and most inaccessible hospitals which nobody else wanted. Stripped of all possessions and privacy individuals are quickly transformed from unique personalities into patients. In Britain it is well known that both for the mentally handicapped as well as for the elderly dependent we have concentrated far more on rehabilitation and activity programmes and not nearly enough on building the right kind of environment. Jean Vanier believes that the environment of the true community is such that hope is found when men and women, whether able or disabled, live together in such a way that growth is really possible. He told us,

Many of the people we have welcomed in our L'Arche communities have come from huge asylums or bad institutions, from the streets or from difficult family situations. Most of them come to us quite wounded, closed up in themselves, sometimes even violent. However, as they gradually discover that they are respected, appreciated and loved, an amazing transformation happens in them. To witness that transformation gives me great hope.

In L'Arche we are discovering the truth of Paul's words that God has chosen the weak and foolish of this world to confound the powerful and the wise. Another fundamental Gospel for us is Luke 14, verse 15, where Jesus tells about a man who gave a great banquet. He invited a number of people but they all refused because they were too busy. They were not bad people; perhaps they were quite virtuous, regularly attending the synagogue, even doing nice things for the poor, but they were too preoccupied to 'waste time' at the banquet. So the man sends out his servants to invite 'the poor, the crippled, the blind and the lame' . . . people with handicaps. And they come running! Why? Because they have time. But more fundamentally because of their deepest yearning to be loved. People who are weak and broken are not interested in knowledge or success or power or even money; they are looking for someone who will say to them: 'You are important. I believe in you. I love you. You are my brother, my sister.' Yes, what the weak, the broken and the lonely are crying out for fundamentally is a friend.

Something else we discover from people with mental disabilities is that they are not people who live in the past or in the future but are incredibly 'live' to the present moment. Their need for friendship and love is such that if they meet someone who appreciates them a gentle force of love is generated. He went on to say,

Love is not just some passing emotional reality. It is not just *doing* things *for* people. If someone is not valued or respected, feelings of guilt or shame or of being 'no good' rise up in him or her. To love is to *reveal* to a person that she or he is unique, special and worthy of attention. We reveal to another person his/her beauty and value not so much by words as by *the way* we look at, speak to, care for them and respond to their cry. And the power of this love helps people move from a broken self-image to a positive self-image. The quality of love, which is the revelation of a person's hidden beauty, transforms people.

This broken self-image about which Jean speaks is

not the unique preserve of those who are handicapped, it is found in many people who find themselves in despair because of the immensity of the problems that we now face in the world, coupled with what he sees as a breakdown in values. From this we derive a sense of brokenness, we experience living in a broken world in which there is much confusion. One thing is certain, that the Christian understanding about the kingdom of God is that it does not come by a steady graph of progress leading to some utopian state. In fact it is almost the opposite. Jesus' own teachings about the future are about many kinds of ups and downs: 'In the world', he says, 'you will have tribulation.'

So the kingdom of God has a great deal to do with the cross of Christ and the resurrection of Christ, for we understand it as a process by which evil is conquered again and again at the cost of great suffering. This is why Jean Vanier believes that there is also a real difference between positive thinking and hope. There may be many good and useful elements in being a positive thinker, but it can be illusory – leading one to believe that although the house is burning everything in fact is fine. Human beings on the whole are scared stiff about the reality of suffering so it is far easier to hide behind temporary illusions of success. Yet in spite of its brokenness the world does in fact offer us many images of hope to reflect on. One such image that Jean finds particularly powerful is that of the vine. He told us,

> I love looking at grapevines in the middle of winter. It looks as if there is no more life in them. As you walk through a vineyard, all you see is dirty stumps of old wood! But then, just three months later, from

that dead wood, new, green life is sprouting forth. I was given a vine which I planted in front of my house. Many people told me they thought it had not taken, that it was dying. And when I touched it, the branches seemed to be falling off. But believe it or not, in the spring leaves started coming out. For me the image of hope is all that mystery around death and new life!

It is this same kind of transformation that can happen in individuals, releasing the whole reality of tenderness, gentleness and openness. He went on to say,

When people are in despair they are closed up in themselves; they do not sense any hope. When we feel alone or if we have been wounded and broken, we tend to close up in our misery, anger and disappointment. But as soon as we sense that we are loved and respected, that there is a meaning to our lives, there is hope. And the fruit of hope is openness. This openness happens in the deepest part of our being as life begins to flow through the cracks. The deepest yearning in the heart of each one of us is for communion, a communion of hearts, the to-and-fro of love, mutual acceptance. And in this communion of hearts I believe there is a real presence of Jesus.

This phrase 'communion of hearts' which Jean introduces into the conversation is another very beautiful way of describing community. Yet this also led us on to reflect that whilst life in community can bring growth through mutual acceptance, there is a cost factor. Elsewhere Jean has written,

Community life brings a painful revelation of our

limitations, weaknesses and darkness; the unexpected discovery of the monsters within us is
hard to accept. The immediate reaction is to try
to destroy the monsters, or to hide them away,
pretending they don't exist . . . But if we accept the
monsters are there, we can let them out and learn
to tame them. That is growth towards liberation.
(*Community and Growth*, DLT, 1989)

From the days of the early Church, Christians found
themselves living in the context of fellow Christians,
not as a community of the righteous (even if some did
get hold of the wrong end of the stick!), but as a
company of those who believed themselves to be for-
given. This may be another way of our understanding
the monsters that need letting out and taming. It
doesn't take long, for instance, for those who are
attracted to come and work in L'Arche communities to
find just how deeply ingrained are their own prejudices:

When assistants arrive in our communities they are
often filled with the prejudices of a competitive
society to which they belong. Then they live and
work and enter into relationship with our people
with mental handicaps, in all their weakness, brokenness, gentleness and their cry for friendship. They
realise more fully the intolerance, lack of love, in
them and in society. They realise more fully that
each person is important, unique, 'holy ground';
each has a specific gift to bring to others. They
realise their own poverty and gifts. Prejudices fall,
truth rises up. We are all fundamentally the same.
Our basic needs are the same as those of all other
human beings. We need others who will call out in

us what is most beautiful, just as we call forth what is most beautiful in others.

It is then through vulnerability, openness and as we break through our own prejudices that the presence of God is deeply known. This led Jean to reflect further with us on the mystery of God's own being. Is it possible for instance for God to feel unloved?

In Jesus is revealed the mystery of God who is love, a Lover. Love is meant to be communicated. If God is not wanted, if people refuse that love, then there is a terrible wound in the heart of God. God is like a wounded lover. A wounded lover is one who wants to give him or her self to another, to live a communion of hearts, but feels rejected. When we love we become more vulnerable and can be hurt if our love is not received. So I believe there is a mystery of littleness, vulnerability and pain in God. Many today reject God, because God does not fix things as we would like.

But many of us are gradually discovering the silence and the littleness of God. God, the all-powerful one, becomes powerless, a God seeking to love, yearning for a heart-to-heart relationship and mutual vulnerability with each one of us: 'You live in me and I live in you.'

God is so little; God does not want to impose on us but has a deep respect for our freedom.

It is interesting to see how Peter was attracted to a powerful Jesus who performed miracles, healed people, etc. and so he was completely broken and scandalised by the powerlessness of Jesus at the cross. It's incredible to read in the Gospel of Matthew how Peter screamed and cursed: 'I do not

know that man!' And in a way it was t ⌐
not know a weak Jesus.

So often it would appear that we are drawn
vulnerable God, but to the God of power,
who will put things right. Indeed it might be ___ that
there is a tendency for the Church to become somewhat
dazzled by the idea of success, which led Jean on to
say,

> Like Peter we too are often looking for a powerful
> Jesus, a powerful Church. We want to have power,
> even if it is to get rid of suffering and weakness
> and to put order into the apparent chaos. Many
> people today are seeking security and are attracted
> to strong movements whether they be political,
> religious, sects, or whatever. We forget that Jesus is
> hidden in the pain and the littleness of our
> humanity.
>
> When we are confronted with crisis, breakages,
> death, divorce, these are crucial moments because
> then we become more conscious of the reality of
> our own lives and of the life of society and of the
> Church. Moments of crisis and breakages are vital
> in our growth in faith, in wholeness and in maturity.
> We discover that the Church, that God, is not an
> ideal. We meet Jesus hidden in the 'mud' of pain
> and of weakness, the reality of God who is not
> seeking power, but who is vulnerable, seeking our
> hearts, to live in communion with us.

At this point we wondered what passages of Scripture Jean felt particularly spoke to him:

> I love the incredible story about the man who was
> born blind and whom Jesus heals. The disciples ask

us whether the blindness of this man was because of his sins or the sins of his parents. Being blind then meant one was guilty; it was a punishment from God! So this blind man was marginalised, cut off from the rest of Jewish society. When he meets Jesus, Jesus heals him. The religious leaders question the formerly blind man again and again to find out what happened. The man is incredibly truthful, so truthful that finally he ends up marginalised again and pushed out of the synagogue! People who have been wounded and pushed aside can sometimes be so incredibly truthful and free.

A few years ago our whole community went on pilgrimage to Rome. We had an audience with the Pope. When he got up to speak to us, Fabio, a man with quite profound mental handicaps, clumsily wandered over to the Pope's chair and sat down! There was a ripple of concern in the group, but Fabio was very much at ease! Like the blind man whom Jesus healed, Fabio had great freedom; he did not care what others thought of him . . . and he had the best chair!

Another incredible gospel story for me is in the Gospel of John. One of the first things Jesus does with his new disciples is to take them to a wedding feast! Why? Because the kingdom of God is like a wedding feast. Then he gradually brings them into places of pain. The first is the woman of Samaria, rejected, marginalised, part of what was considered a sectarian group. Then they touch the pain of a father who has lost his son. After that he takes them to what I call the local psychiatric hospital, the pool of Bethsaida, where there was a crowd of broken, paralysed, blind and infirm people. Often what strikes people most when they read this passage is the miraculous healing. What strikes me most is that Jesus would bring his disciples straight away to this place of mass pain, so that the disciples come in contact with people in pain and discover that their role is to announce the Good News to the poor who will be transformed by that Good News.

Another very meaningful passage for us in L'Arche is when Jesus says: 'When you give a lunch or a dinner, do not invite your family members nor your rich neighbours . . . but when you give a banquet, invite the poor, the crippled, the lame and the blind and you will be blessed' (Luke 14:12–14). The blessing is eating at the same table as the poor – the mystery of God calling us to oneness. The pain of God, in spite of all the divisions of race, culture, class and abilities, is to help people recognise each other's gifts. God yearns for unity, to bring all of humanity into one body. This text is about eating around the same table with people who are very different and becoming friends. If we do that, we receive a blessing of God. I believe this is what Christianity is all about: we discover Jesus so that we can discover Jesus in each other with their gifts, their beauty, their limits and their difference.

We then asked Jean what is the greatest sign of hope that he sees in the Church as we approach the new millennium. He told us,

What I see in the churches today is an openness to difference. We are moving away from churches seen

35

as fortresses with walls around them. The old walls are beginning to crack because we realise that we need each other; the powers of destruction are so immense. These could be the powers of the mafia, of drugs, of atomic warfare, of violence, of multi-nationals that crush individuals or all the forces of destruction on our planet. We are beginning to see this communion between Christians of different traditions and even between people of different religions. There is a whole underlying movement in the hearts of many people which is a search for unity and peace and for me this is the greatest hope. We are beginning to see that we all belong to a common humanity, that if we do not work together it will be the suicide of the whole of humanity. But if we come together, if we respect and love each other, then we can do something beautiful.

For that we need to let ourselves be touched by the Holy Spirit. What are the signs of the Spirit? A new freedom, the freedom in order to love: 'You were called to be free; do not use your freedom as an opening for self-indulgence, but be servants of one another in love' (Galatians 5:13). We are moving into a new and exciting era. Something totally new is being given, where we no longer rest upon laws and power or everybody being good and great but where we are discovering together a new, mysterious presence of God.

One important step that congregations can take towards becoming a sign of hope is to rediscover a strong sense of community built with a real respect for weakness and difference, seeking, not always perfectly, to live out the transforming love and justice that flows out of Jesus' life, death and resurrection. It will take us to new heights and depths in our understanding of mutual acceptance and, as we also discover, it is a critical element in our approach to evangelism. For what we are seeking to become is a place where those who are searching for meaning and friendship, are attracted because they find a community dependable and loving. Just becoming part of that community feels like coming home. Indeed without too much searching we know that in every congregation there are needs that can summon compassion, forgiveness and acceptance. That is an invitation in itself! The question is not, 'Do we have the resources to become that kind of community?' but 'Do we have the resolve and the motivation?'

Suggestions for Further Reading
Other books by Jean Vanier:
   Man and Woman He Made Them (DLT, 1985)
   The Broken Body (DLT, 1988)
   Community and Growth (DLT, 1989)
   Tears of Silence (DLT, 1991)
   Jesus the Gift of Love (Hodder and Stoughton, 1994)
   Our Journey Home (Hodder and Stoughton, 1997)
   The Scandal of Service (DLT, 1997)

GROUP WORK

Reminder: These are suggested questions. Please feel free to be selective, to adapt them or to make up some of your own.
  1. Describe some of the ways that your church

community could be said to be 'a home of the homeless'. What more could you do to increase the experience of 'loving acceptance'?

2. With the closure of so many large psychiatric institutions, the government has provided 'Care in the Community'. What are the fears this has aroused? What positive steps could your church take to support 'Care in the Community'?

3. 'Love is . . . to reveal to a person that she or he is unique, special and worthy of attention.' In what ways have you experienced and been helped to move from a 'broken self-image' to a 'positive self-image'? (p. 28)

4. Why is it that human beings are 'scared stiff about the reality of suffering'? (p. 29) As disciples of Christ how could we speak about the mystery of suffering to those who find it meaningless?

5. Jean Vanier speaks about the 'grapevines in the middle of winter' (p. 29) as being a powerful image of hope for him. What images from the world could you describe that speak to you of the mystery of death and life?

6. What is your experience of prejudice in the church community? How can we become more a 'communion of hearts' that is described on page 30?

7. In our worship we often use the language of 'God Almighty' which might sound as though God can 'fix everything'. What can we understand and learn from the vulnerability of Jesus? What does that say about the nature of God? What difference does that make to the way we relate to each other? (pp. 32–3)

8. If God is 'hidden in the "mud" of pain and of weakness' (p. 33) how is he revealed?

9. How does your church value difference? (pp. 35–6) What are the different gifts your church values and how could they be said to transform the community?
10. What evidence do you find for an underlying movement in humanity for unity? Who are the groups that we would search with, or not search with, and why?

Encountering Scripture

The parable of the Wedding Banquet in Luke's Gospel is about a man whose invitation to his guests to come to the wedding feast is refused. Those invited all have sensible reasons not to accept. At the end of the story the kind host is angry, saying that those who refused will never taste of his supper. In their place he has invited the local riff-raff – the sort of people we might call 'life's losers'. In a sense they would have had far more reason to make excuses since they would have felt out of place. His parable turns our idea of salvation on its head. It is saying that we are saved not because we are good, honest, hardworking people, clawing our way into the kingdom by our own success, but through God's grace which works on untouchable, unacceptable humanity. In other words you have to be as good as dead and let God be God in you and for you. This is underlined by Jesus' saying that the only way to find life is to lose it!

Read Luke 14:12–24.

In what ways does your church community classify those who are 'in' and those who are 'out' – those who are welcome to the table and those who are not?

Where and why do we draw the line?

Do we treat others in the way that we have been treated by a gracious God?

In the church we have all kinds of resources. Do we use them to build up relationships and friendships?

Does the way the church deals with money help or hinder a real sense of belonging? Are there dangers around in some of the methods of fundraising which might make some people feel like second-class citizens? How might these be addressed?

You may like to use this prayer at the end of your discussion. First spend a few moments reflecting quietly on what you have been talking about and helping each other discover.

Lord Jesus, as you call us to follow you
help us to understand that we shall not always
know whether we are to walk alone or with
another.
But if we put our roots down with broken and
little people
the path we take will become clearer.
That we shall discover the fundamental meaning
of our lives,
the secret of Jesus hidden in brokenness.
Teach us what it means to be human
that we can live with people very different
from one another and from ourselves.
Help us to be a sign
of the value of each person
no matter how poor
no matter how broken

so that people may discover for themselves
the saving power of the gospel.
Amen.

A Different Way of Seeing

Becoming communities that break down
some of the barriers between the material
and the spiritual

with Kathy Galloway

An American woman theologian once commented on the Church something like this: 'A strange thing happened on the way to worship today. The vibrant people of God turned into an institution.' For all of us at times, the Church as an institution can feel frustrating. What we want to happen is hindered if not completely stopped by what seems to be Church bureaucracy. We throw our hands up in frustration and ask, 'What hope is there for the Church when it stops all I want to do?' However, the times are changing.

Over the past thirty years or so God has been empowering lay people to discover a fresh understanding of what it means to be the people of God. Across all Church boundaries, in young, middle-aged and elderly people, inside and outside denominations, there has been an awakening. In consequence we delight in new worship, new expressions of belief and new insights into how we might live together. This movement was not begun in any one country. It is a consequence of a much larger movement around the world which has emerged from God's blessing on the poor.

Some communities, notably in South America, Africa and Asia, have paved the road of hope for western Christians. To explore what these types of communities are saying to us today we interviewed Revd Kathy Galloway, one time Warden of Iona Abbey, a member of the Iona Community, author of many titles and at present a member within Lansdowne Parish Church in Glasgow.

Many people will know of, or even might have tasted the fruits of, the Iona Community from which much music, poetry and new insights into expressing worship have become part of regular church experience. Old, sometimes ancient, truths are given new life, arresting the listener and enabling new meaning, but is this what Iona is all about? We asked Kathy first of all what she was trying to achieve whilst on Iona.

I think that on Iona we were attempting to be a place for the common life and to embody the concerns and the priorities of the Community, for the breaking down of the barriers between the material and the spiritual. The Church in Britain has suffered for a long time from a kind of dualism that has rendered part of people's life and experience as spiritual, holy, good, and another part of it as bad and secular and not holy. Therefore it's had the effect of separating people from themselves.

In the past, politics has often been seen as bad or dirty but prayer was seen as all right. George Macleod, who was the founder of the Iona Community, was always very trenchant about these things. He's famously quoted as having said that it was blasphemous to pray for Mary with bronchitis if you were not also prepared to take action to do something about the damp housing that was causing her bronchitis. He used very strong language – 'blasphemous'. It's rather like Isaiah when he says, 'Stop all your noisy shouting, I hate your religious festivals!'

So Iona is about the expression of a rebuilding, of a reintegration of the life of both the individual and the corporate, the personal and the political, the spiritual and the material, trying to build up many of the connections that have been severed.

Iona is a place steeped in history but this modern expression of community that Iona demonstrates has its roots not so long ago. We asked Kathy where and when that began.

Originally it came out of the experience of Glasgow during the Depression, in particular the shipyards during that Depression. George Macleod, in his ministry in the dock area, found that people who were unemployed, who were poor, who were struggling and wanting the church to be able to communicate with them felt totally removed from the church. Their experience and their perception was that it was for respectable people, for good people, and they didn't really fit. There was such a division between the church and the community.

So I think that it stemmed from the actual experience of people, but was moved by the contemplation of Jesus, by a very strong sense of the incarnation, that Jesus became a human being. The word became flesh, not just more words. By assuming humanness, Jesus made humanness holy. There's no part of human life that we can say is not valid or precious and we are not in the business of saving souls. Our vocation is to the whole person, not just to disembodied souls. The notion of souls without bodies is nonsense, I mean you can't disembody people in that way.

George Macleod began in the shipyards of Glasgow amongst the poor but not all of us live in such situations. In fact we all live in a unique place with its own particularity. So what is it that the Iona Community can say to each of these diverse places that we live in?

People come from very different starting points

and I think that very often they are looking for something. They have a sense of dissatisfaction, a sense of disconnection. They are looking for belonging and community. Sometimes there's a tendency to want to look up and out in very high places. I suppose that my sense would be much more just to look where you are. I think it's more to do with seeing what's actually round about in a different way. It's not seeing different things, it's seeing the same things in a different way. Incarnational spirituality is about attempting to see and discovering people with the eyes of love. That, I think, gives you a different way of relating to the world. One doesn't always see people in that way! Sometimes, one has to work hard at it – but then also it's a gift, it's a paradox, it's grace.

We went on to talk about the world in which we live and how we perceive it. It could be said that we live in a very measurement orientated world where business is measured in terms of profit, schools in terms of their inspections, hospitals by their recovery rates and even churches in terms of how many people attend. From one point of view there's nothing wrong with measuring growth. Children love to measure their height or what they can do now, as compared with a year ago. We encourage that, but sometimes people are measured by what they can (or more often what they can't) do without regard to who they are inside.

I think that the trend in our society is to judge by external things. It's one of the consequences of living in a free market society. We use the values of the market to judge people and if you have a philosophy that adds value according to people's market desirability or adds value according to marketability, it's only a very small step to do that to people as well.

The market operates on the principle that things are more valuable, that they command a higher price, the more rare, the more beautiful, the more unusual, the more exotic they are; correspondingly, lower prices are given for what's ordinary, or there's plenty of, or what's unglamorous.

I think that if you're old, or if you're very young, if you're vulnerable in some way, if you're imperfect, or if you're damaged, society values you less. For me that's profoundly *ungospel*. It's not the gospel because the gospel is about the absolute intrinsic value of people. Everybody, no matter who they are or what they've done or what they're like, is loved, is precious. So in a sense you go against the cultural tide to try and see the intrinsic rather than the extrinsic worth of people. A real danger for the Church at the moment is that it becomes too caught up in extrinsic value, in the Church's marketability or image rather than in its faithfulness.

So often damage or vulnerability or imperfection is seen as failure in our society and failure is not a comfortable word. Decline in membership, lack of influence in the community, internal arguments in the Church all serve to lower morale and even make some people reject it. We need to find a way to cope with failure. But how?

To begin with, I don't think that the Church is very good at understanding failure, which is most peculiar, if you think about it, because that's what the gospel is so much about. We don't like the notion of failure and it's very hard for people to admit it. One of the things that makes community-building most difficult within the church is the lack of ability to be honest and vulnerable with one another. In a way, the more successful the church or the more successful the neighbourhood, the harder it is.

My experience has been that the church can be most the church where it's in the most vulnerable positions. People can't be defensive any more. If you're very poor or if you are living in a community that has a huge stigma attached to it, you can't be defensive any longer. You have to depend on one another. You have to be able to be vulnerable and it's only on that level that sharing really starts.

Sometimes I think that actually more failure would be good for the Church! The point of breaking, or the point of pain, or the point of failure, is also the point of growth. One of the things that I think people really struggle with, and it's part of a yearning, is the experience of grace. For me, so much of the gospel Good News is about the experience of grace, unthought, undeserved, and uncontrolled. That takes you to a very different place, whereas so often we seem to be stuck with people's perceptions of the Church being about moral codes or morality. My feeling is that Christianity, or the gospel, really starts where morality gives out, fails, stops. It's what you do when things break down. It's what happens when people don't behave the way they should. It's what happens when you have enemies, when people do hurtful things. These seem to me places where faith really starts.

A movement that has known a struggle for grace this century is feminism. Some would say the struggle is not over and women's gifts and experience are still not valued in the Church. Of course it differs from church to church. In some it is very evident, in others less so. We asked Kathy how she sees women's gifts and experience valued within the Church and how the Church might do more.

I think it's a lot better now than it has been. Obviously, the Church is affected by movements in society and also maybe to some extent plays a part in shaping these. There's no doubt at all that the gifts of women have been undervalued in the past and taken for granted and abused horribly, and that women themselves have often internalised a low opinion of themselves based on that. I think that's changing. The ordination of women, which is by no means a universal panacea for every woman, is an important step.

I value a much greater diversity of ministry and of witness for women, who were terribly confined into a narrow space. I think it's very interesting, looking at society generally. If the constraints are taken off women and they are given encouragement, they actually prove themselves very competent in all sorts of fields. The other side of that is that it offers a lot of possibilities to men as well, to extend the range of what's possible. It's good not to have such narrow channels for people, but to value the diversity of human gift and experience.

As to putting that into practice, I think that there's a real problem in the Church which is not just rooted in gender but it's rooted in the role of lay and clergy. We are not very good at valuing the skills and the gifts of lay people generally. We are not very good at seeing churches as a body, we have such a hangover from the past, of the minister or the priest or the vicar being the church and then everyone else helping them.

I'm someone who strongly believes in liturgy as 'the work of the people'. The clergy task is to be an enabler, almost a midwife, helping new things to come to birth, helping people to find new skills, new creativity, new possibilities, both individually and corporately. Therefore, for me, training is important, equipping people to be the church, and to be the church in the world and not just the church in the Church.

The Iona Community was like that for me, although I think it's also in my upbringing. I grew up in a local church where the gifts of lay people were extremely valued in worship, in pastoral work, in community leadership, in a whole range of different ways, in our housing estate parish, in a working-class area. The level of confidence and maturity that people gained as a result was quite significant for me.

You see, the church is not the clergy, the church is the whole people of God and we cannot go on infantilising people. We have to recognise their strengths. I find it extraordinary sometimes that the church has this desire to keep people permanently adolescent, or even infant. We should be much more encouraging of people's theological questions and doubts and struggles if we want people to grow up spiritually in faith. We have this notion of Jesus as being somebody who went around giving answers but actually he went around much more asking questions. All the time Jesus asked people questions, 'Who do you say that I am?', 'Whose face is on the coin?' 'You decide'. Putting the responsibility of decision back to people and trusting them.

There's a wonderful story that George Macleod used to tell about Jesus ascending into heaven and the Angel Gabriel talking to Jesus, a bit concerned, and saying, 'Lord, you've left your work on earth. You've left it in the hands of these fishermen and housewives and tax collectors, are you not a bit concerned about it? Do you not feel that they're not theologically trained, or not ordained? They're not great intellectuals, they've not got degrees, are you not worried about it?' And Jesus looks at Gabriel and says, 'I have no other plans'.

I'm surprised that people take it, take being patronised, but of course there are a lot of people who don't. A lot of people just go. They leave because this is the only part of their lives where they are treated as children. That's not a healthy model. I have a biblical image of what I think the church should look like. It's of the vine and the branches. All of that fifteenth chapter from John's Gospel, not servants but friends, is about mutuality and reciprocity and respect.

Learning how to respect one another and finding a mutually civilised way of living is what true politics is about. Yet that word has come to be a problem for some who belong to the Church and for some who don't want the Church meddling in politics. There are those who feel a too radical Church easily loses its sense of the God it worships and would rather it stuck to religious matters. Yet the experience of those who are oppressed is often that if the Church does not speak up and act out its religion it is not worth a listen. Kathy has been involved in a lot of political campaigning, primarily in anti-poverty organisations, but also in the campaign for a Scottish parliament. She worked for a short time for the Scottish Constitutional Convention which drew up the blueprint for the parliament. Within that she was also involved in a group which was working to ensure that women's rights and possibilities were well represented within the plans. We asked her how possible it is to put the gospel and politics together.

For me, the hard thing is to separate them, not to put them together. Scotland is a political culture, the separation between politics and religion is much less the case in Scotland than it is in England. People are used to the Church's involvement in politics. We have a huge history of it, all the way from Mary Queen of Scots right through the nineteenth century. People take it quite for granted, for example, that industrial chaplains will mediate in industrial disputes or that you would expect the Churches to speak out on various political matters. For example, during the Gulf War, the most organised and the most coherent opposition came from the Churches and from the trade unions and this is quite a strong partnership in Scotland, I would say.

For me, it's also biblical. Isaiah says, 'Truth stumbles in the market place and justice finds no place there. God sees this and is astonished that there's no one there to help the weak.' It's such a political call to action and that's not to say party political. However, there's a kind of neurosis about the word 'political'. Politics is just how we organise our care collectively. I find it really odd that people should find it strange or threatening that as soon as the gospel grows from, 'it's all right to help your neighbour', to become a plan to help a group of neighbours, it's considered political and dangerous. I find that quite inexplicable!

One explanation might be to do with the fear of not knowing who our neighbours are. In the story of the Good Samaritan Jesus challenges us with the question 'Who shall we be a neighbour to?' By this he redefines our responsibilities, so that we are asked to act in a neighbourly way to others. Rather than wait for neighbours to come to us, we take the initiative. *Faith in the City*, an Anglican report on inner city life, attempted to take that initiative and by doing so raised the profile of inner city areas, housing schemes and estates. Kathy works in one of the major cities in Britain so we asked her about what kind of hope she sees there and how hope is maintained.

I think very often inner cities are terribly misrepresented and people are quite ignorant about what they are like. People have a kind of image of no-go areas and wild children. So much of it is completely distorted because partly it's based on police experience, which is only with a section of the community, and so much is based on media coverage, where people rush in and spend ten minutes covering a story.

There's a real demonisation of people who live on housing schemes and estates. People are categorised as the underclass or ghettoised in all sorts of ways. Then of course it means you can justify all sorts of things, all sorts of political action. My experience of housing estates is that the vast majority of people are people of ability and pride. The fact is that people there are poor. It's not that there's anything else wrong with them. When people are poor, their choices are more limited in all sorts of ways. Being poor should not be a crime, but it's in danger of being seen in that way.

In terms of hope, I think it's a great sign of hope that our inner cities are not burning in flames, because they're symptoms and symbols of profound injustice and of a philosophy which treats people as disposable. There are people living on housing estates in our cities in Britain who have actually been rendered completely redundant to the economy because they don't have capital. Their labour, because it's unskilled, has a low value and because they're poor they have no value as consumers. They're actually irrelevant to the economy and when you feel you're irrelevant, you feel that you have no worth. It's hard to sustain hope; and the fact that so many people do so is an extraordinary tribute.

In terms of hope in local churches, I think of a church that I worked in recently in North Lanarkshire. It is set in a kind of post-industrial blighted landscape in the shadow of Ravenscraig, a steel plant – and then the steel went. The people in that church have turned their church into a neighbourhood centre. They looked at what it meant to address the needs of their community, what it meant to be a neighbour and they did that very interestingly, using the tools of Latin American liberation theology. They applied these tools and that way of thinking to a Scottish context, very intentionally and in a very disciplined way.

They weren't too proud to say that they could learn from Nicaraguan peasants. They had no sense of themselves as being other than or over against their community. What they did was to take some empowerment back into their lives, to make decisions about their community *in* the community and not to have them made for them by professionals.

One of the things that is really strong about local churches is that they actually have the capacity to make and carry out decisions locally. Very often people are in a situation where the decisions about many things in their life, about education, about health, about social care, about culture, are taken for them by others. The extent of people's involvement in them is their vote and then their representatives will take these decisions. People who are not actually living in the community will take these decisions.

Local churches have an enormous opportunity, because in some situations they are the only collective expression of the local interests, or local concerns. I would love to be able to see the church being a more supportive network and to see it actually believe it is one body. Often churches are in competition with each other. However, there are huge signs of hope where people are able to see themselves as the community. They don't see themselves as the church which has answers for the community, they see themselves as being part of the community which has questions.

Kathy spoke about the need for unity yet so often the institutional Church finds this hard. When we say we believe in *one* holy, catholic and apostolic Church, in what sense is our belief a vague hope or a present reality? The creed is one of our institutional formulas, a kind of constitution of the Church. Putting it into practice, though, in and across the institutional barriers, is another thing. Kathy has worked in the World Council of Churches which seeks to bring about a greater ecumenism, a means by which Christians can live, work and be together. But this isn't easy:

I think there's a difficulty in the ecumenical movement and sometimes people get a bit despairing about it. Personally I feel that this is because they are looking in the wrong places. If you look at the institution of the Church for your signs of hope you would get kind of despairing. But it's like an iceberg. There's the tip that you can see and then there's the bit that's submerged, the bit where people just get on with things locally. They don't necessarily do them with ecumenical labels, they just do them because they're the things that need doing.

I live in Glasgow. Fifty years ago and even thirty years ago, Catholics and Protestants killed each other in Glasgow. They don't do that now. That, for me, is the first and most important thing about the ecumenical movement, so that people won't kill each other, so that people learn to value and respect each other's perspective and faith. I don't have a lot of patience when I think that there's a lack of respect or a lack of tolerance of difference. As Christians, if we can't allow people to be different, if we have to make people the same, then it seems to me that it's an absolute negation of Christianity. Christianity is about living with people and loving people though we are different.

Finally Kathy spoke about her own expressions of hope within herself and in particular about her writing.

I think that prayer and poetry and art and song are very important to me. I suppose again it's a part of my tradition. I think as a writer, as a poet. I'm a poet through my feet, because I feel the rhythm, it comes through my feet first. It's to do with being connected with the earth and a lot of the Iona Community songs and the 'Wild Goose' songs shape my inner landscape. I suppose that they're the music inside my head in a way. John and Graham and I, and many others, wrote a lot because when we were trying to describe the experience of community we were trying to find words for prayer, particularly I think for intercession. We didn't write out of inspiration, we wrote out of desperation.

This song, 'Inspired by Love and Anger', is one that really moves me, partly because it has one of these wonderful Irish tunes (all the best tunes come from Ireland originally!), partly because the words speak of both love and anger. There's a kind of passion that says, 'OK, you don't have to be polite, you don't have to be respectable, what you have to do is love and be angry and turn that anger into constructive action'.

I have a passion for justice, a passion for poetry and a passion for people and we live in a world where there are so many injustices that it's funny to find that, in a sense, hopeful.

This verse is what my faith struggles to be.

God asks who will go for me,
  who will extend my reach,
and who when few will listen,
  will prophecy and preach,
and who when few bid welcome,
  will offer all they know,
and who when few dare follow,
  will walk the road I show.
(by John L. Bell and Graham Maule,
©WRRG Iona Community)

Suggestions for Further Reading
By Kathy Galloway:
Struggles to Love: the Spirituality of the Beatitudes (SPCK, 1994)
Talking to the Bones (SPCK, 1996)
Starting Where We Are (Wild Goose Publications)
A Story to Live By (SPCK, 1998)

GROUP WORK

Reminder: These are suggested questions. Please feel free to be selective, adapt them or make up some of your own.

1. In what ways in your church community have you found God 'empowering lay people to discover a fresh understanding of what it means to be the

people of God'? Give specific examples. How does your worship together truly reflect this empowerment?

2. Kathy refers to the barriers between the material and the spiritual (p. 46). How might some of these barriers be broken down?

3. Does your church community have diversity or does it feel as if it is for respectable, good people?

4. What do you count as success in your church? How do you cope with failure? (pp. 49–50)

5. What does Kathy mean when she says that 'the gospel really starts where morality gives out, fails, stops'? (p. 50)

6. How does your church community value or not value the contribution of women?

7. What evidence in your church is there of shared ministry? Does it feel as if there are 'the few who do' and 'the many who don't'?

8. Jot down three or four things that you would like to experience as a result of being a regular attender at your church. Compare and discuss your lists. Are there overlaps? How could your worship be changed to reflect these needs?

9. Was there a time when the church failed to meet your needs? Can you share this experience with your group?

10. From your own experience, what are some of the most difficult issues to be found in your local neighbourhood? What could your church contribute to addressing them?

11. Is there a danger that the church could become an extension of the social services? What could it offer that is distinctively different and life-giving?

12. What areas of training could you use to help equip

you as a church to be more conscious of your vocation in the world?

13. 'Learning how to respect one another and finding a mutually civilised way of living is what true politics is about . . . [but] some don't want the church meddling in politics' (p. 53). In the light of this you might like to consider these phrases from the Lord's Prayer:

> Your will be done on earth as in heaven.
> Give us this day our daily bread.

What happens when these words are not seen to have a political dimension?

14. What opportunities are there for you to help shape public opinion in your everyday life? How can you help to clear up misunderstandings about Christ and the Church with its message of peace and justice?

Encountering Scripture

Solomon was one of the kings in Jerusalem, who was respected for his wise judgements. He had in his life asked for one gift from God, namely a heart to understand how to govern the people and how 'to discern between good and evil' (1 Kings 3:4–15). Psalm 72 is dedicated to him and it begins by speaking of the real needs of the poor against a background of injustice and oppression in the land. It then moves towards an idealised picture of how things should be – a time of peace, expressed in that lovely word 'shalom', and prosperity for all.

Read Psalm 72 slowly, reflecting on its words, pictures and hopes.

After a short time of quiet, you might like to consider as a group how the sentiments expressed in the Psalm apply to those who rule today.

What unjust practices are you aware of in your own community?

What action could the church take to address them?

What might be the first practical steps that could be taken?

You might like to end this session by listening to the song that Kathy sings and follow it with a time of quiet reflection.

Session 4

The Community of Faith

Becoming communities that live openly
and honestly with difficult issues

with Jim Thompson

The first thing that impresses you when you meet Bishop Jim is his amazing capacity for hope. He has been Bishop of Bath and Wells since 1991 and is a well-known author and broadcaster who can often be heard on the BBC's *Thought for the Day*. For Bishop Jim, hope is born out of the single conviction that the whole universe has come into existence not through some cosmic accident (because, he contends, if it has then it proceeds into chaos) but with a purpose and a design demonstrated in Christ. Of course once you have said that, there are those awkward and difficult questions which have to be wrestled with: about suffering and waste and how these somehow fit into the divine scheme of things. For some people, the changing and unpredictable nature of creation is not only difficult to accept but in itself leads them ultimately to despair, death and meaninglessness.

However, Bishop Jim finds the universe totally awe-inspiring. It is this sense of wonderment which has led him over the years to contemplate the mysterious nature of the Creator. He acknowledges that science and religion have often been in conflict with each other but he believes that this has largely arisen through misunderstanding. The Bible was never meant to be a scientific book, with answers to questions that could never have been asked, especially in the creation narratives in Genesis. These narratives in Scripture are the way in which a developing faith community through story, legend and poetry sought to interpret history and understand *why* things came into existence rather than *how*. The human quest for truth will always be fascinated with the question of 'how': How did the universe come into existence? How was it made? and so on. But it is when we ask questions about whether the universe has any meaning that we can with integrity say it is not unreasonable to believe in a Creator. Moreover, this Creator is not some sort of anonymous power but has a personality and a passionate concern for the creation which could in the Genesis story only be described as good.

Hope also springs from the fact that Christians believe in a Creator who has shown himself to us in Christ and that through Christ we can, in a very intimate sense, be in relationship with the Creator. This gives us hope, but it doesn't mean that we are totally freed from the struggles and not sometimes despairing of life. He told us:

> I think that hope is what keeps us going. It's a great energy. In one sense optimists on the face of it are more likely to be hopeful, because they think everything is going to turn out all right in the end. There is a bit of that in me! I think optimists and pessimists are very much who they are by character. But Christian hope is not like that, because there may be very real turmoil and struggles to go through. Sometimes, hope has been at its most powerful where things have been at their most impossible. So hope, in Christian terms, is based profoundly on the realities that are around us now. I do think that hope *now* is the important thing. The future is a different matter. Of course it involves the future – in other words the hope is partly that things will get better. But they may not get better in this life. Sometimes the hope is the heavenly hope. I guess that the reason why so many slaves had hope in the face of their own lives was

because they saw it as one step towards that kingdom which is free of all those human evils.

He then went on to remind us that St Paul had spoken of the three great virtues – faith, hope and love. St Paul had chosen love as the greatest, although that may not have been an easy choice. Faith and hope are just as essential to a wholeness in life. In fact it was this virtue that had been so important for the Bishop at a time much earlier in his life when he felt very despairing about himself:

> My faith grew out of a time of feeling hopeless about myself. God gave me hope about myself, that I was loveable, that I could become what I wanted to be in the end, that I could have real love in my life. So there is always that personal side to hope – hope about oneself.

Perhaps this idea becomes a little clearer when we think that God is present in every aspect of life, though it has to be said that not every aspect carries the fullness of his presence. This is particularly important for anyone who is tempted to believe that however despairing or hopeless they may feel about themselves there is no aspect of life that does not in a very deep sense carry the whisper of God. He is very present in the hope that every situation can be redeemed. In fact one of the Psalms reminds us that even if we were to make our bed in hell, God would be there lying down with us! So what kind of advice would the Bishop give to people who feel a sense of hopelessness about themselves?

> I think two things about such a situation: one is to listen and wait until hope begins to build in the

person because it's their hope, or their hope from God, that changes the situation. I sometimes think in dealing with very depressed people, even despairing people, that if we have a laugh, I mean, if we get to the point where the person can laugh, I feel that somehow (it's probably completely irrational) we have got somewhere because they have seen that they are still a laughing person. They can still smile at life – even if it is their own misfortune. I think one of the most hopeful things in a way is something that Jesus shows us. It is seeing someone who's looking at you hopeless, feeling hopeless about themselves, with a very low self-image . . . or hopeless about their situation or about the world . . . and Jesus somehow sees through to the potential of the *person*. So that the blind person was not just a blind person but a person and the leper was not just someone with bruised, scarred, bleeding skin, rejected by the whole of society, but was a *person*, a loved person. And as you read the Gospels, you can almost feel people gaining hope.

I think that another source of hope is other people believing in you, other people believing that things can be done. I don't know if you ever watch *EastEnders* but it is amazing how often they say to each other, 'I promise you it will be all right' – *I promise you it will be all right*. You know as it's said that they have no power over the future, it's just total fantasy – but there is hope there. It must be handled with great care, though, because a Christ produced as some sort of magic rabbit out of the hat is not Christ. In fact, that can push people further and further into despair. You see this particularly with someone with a chronic life-threatening disease, say multiple sclerosis. If you say, 'Christ can heal you', then that may be what you believe but it may send that person with multiple sclerosis into an ever-increasing despair about themselves – *I am to blame because I am not better.*

It is important we recognise that Jesus lived in a pre-scientific world. Since then, the healing power of God has been shed abroad in many wonderful, different ways – not least in the development of scientific medicine. Healing now proceeds through both internal and external means in which there is a greater interplay of the social sciences, medicine and compassion. When the Christian community prays for the health and well-being of others it is not because we believe ill-health or disease are the direct result of some wrongdoing in the past, but because it is quite simply a way of loving. We bring the person or situation we are concerned about to God in the knowledge that we are reflecting all that Christ taught us about God's desire for a world in which human beings really care for each other. It is in making that connection that we can then begin to see things happen.

The Bishop went on to reflect on the question of marginalisation. By nature, he could be described as a street fighter – he has always put up a robust defence of those who are discriminated against in any way. If the local church community is to become a sign of hope for marginalised and alienated people, then it must understand that the poor have always occupied a very special place in the purposes of God. Whilst they may be the object of concern for the church community this is not because they are lacking materially or spiritually and have nothing to give or offer. In fact, quite the opposite – as the gospel so often reminds us they can transfigure the community itself as well as the ways in which the community relates to the local situation and to the world at large. Bishop Jim said:

Jesus was always reaching out to the outcast, to the person who was marginalised and I think that has been very central to my own approach to Christianity. In a way I think Jesus has the biggest problem with those who are very self-satisfied, totally in control of things and believe they are right over and against all the rest. There aren't many figures like that in the New Testament that Jesus seems to have been very keen on. In fact he very much challenged that sort of self-righteousness. So it's important to me that he looked to all the characters other people wouldn't have seen value in – Zacchaeus, the woman taken in adultery, Matthew the tax gatherer, Peter the completely chaotic, faithful, loving person. It has been important to bring all that with me as I try to do my ministry and this has meant, in a society of aggressive whites, supporting Bangladeshis who have no homes, whose children have alopecia through their anxiety, or people who everybody scorns.

The homeless especially, I think, are marginalised in so many ways and the Church has a great record in this country. I'm co-president of the English Churches' Housing Group where a very large organisation actually provides almost every sort of home. The range starts from the cold shelters for people to come in from the streets when it's really cold. They are pretty disheartening places – but they are there, they're a roof, they're warm, there's food. It goes right the way through to the restored tramp who's learnt to live on his own strength again, living in a very nice flat and taking a pride in feeling a new person with a new hope. Now there are so many ways that Christians can be involved in this major remaining scandal of our lives.

I could say almost exactly the same about unemployment, which also excludes people. Someone once said that we are becoming more and more a divided society between those who have work and those who don't have work. And there are some people who are learning to live without work at all. So unemployment is something in which Christians should be very much involved.

There are also those who are socially alienated, socially homeless people and they are all around us – and it is not just an urban thing. There are some people who really struggle to survive in rural areas, there is homelessness in rural areas.

But then there is the other sort of homelessness which is the people who are very much lost in the world, isolated, very much alone. I became deeply aware of this when we had nineteen tower blocks in my parish. In the forty-four flats in each tower block you went up in the lift and no one talked to anybody. I was usually the only one who talked to anybody going up in the lift and I think they thought I was a bit mad! But you realised that people die of loneliness, people go for months without being touched by anybody. I believe we all need to be touched and held. To me, Christ is in them and therefore we reach out to him in them.

I think rootlessness and hopelessness would be quite good words to describe much of our society. The Church should be a massive challenge to all that, not just the social exclusion but also the personal, individual, homeless isolation. It's very central to the Christian Faith.

What can we do? I think we have to be much more where people are rather than expect them to come where we are. We are a Church that very much sees our task as bringing people to Church. In all my ministry of thirty odd years this has been very hard, except in those places where somehow it has become a success story. It has been very hard and tough for us all. Maybe the lesson that God has for us in all this is that we have been too interested in fitting people into *our* box. We need to be going where they are, as he did, and meeting their real fears, their real alarms, their discomfort, their jollity, their humour, their realities. Being immersed there, we discover that they are God's children. I think this is difficult for us.

Our interview with Bishop Jim continued immediately after an important debate in his Diocesan Synod on the Church of England's report on 'Issues in Human Sexuality'. Sexuality has always been a notoriously difficult and controversial subject for Christians to discuss and it has to be admitted from the outset that there are no easy answers. We recognise now that the ethical problems raised by sex and sexual activity in human beings cannot be dealt with in isolation, for they concern the whole of an individual's identity.

Ethical issues, in fact, confront us with the complexity of our humanity. It is therefore vital that the world at large sees that the Christian community debates such issues with care and maturity, holding together views that are widely different. As the Bishop observes, though, this is not new:

> I think the first thing to say is the Church has had to face difficult issues and conflicts from the very beginning. The conflict over circumcision, for instance, which maybe to us seems like just a rather strange discussion item was, of course, for the Jews a whole question of their identity and their history and their tradition. To them, that was at least as huge as the issues we find difficult today. And the way they tackled them was in the Council where Paul and Peter and the Apostles talked together and tried to face out the issues. Sometimes they differed so much they parted ways, as when Barnabas left Paul. But the things that they were discussing were very central to their lives. They are not central to ours – the eating of meat offered to idols, the question of circumcision itself were all about their identity now that they were becoming Christians. St Paul was quite clear that the Law, that was the way in which people felt they had to obey a culture or a custom, was not the way to the gospel; it was not obedience to all these things that was the way to the gospel.

When it comes to discussing difficult moral or ethical issues, the key thing is for Christians to be well informed, not to be afraid of an honest debate in an atmosphere of mutual trust and then:

You sit, you pray, you get into a way of thinking that says, 'I'm not going to slag off my neighbour, I'm going to love them whatever they think.' And this is where the Church should be able to offer real resources to the rows and wars which go on in the world. Sometimes unfortunately the Church has made things incomparably worse. We don't have any difficulty thinking of the situations where there have been religious wars ... but that is not as Christ intended. I am sure that Christ intended us to listen to each other, to forgive each other, to respect each other. He calls us to love each other in the Church as he loves the Father and the Father loves him. We are called to a very high standard of human relationships. So to tackle these things we need the debate to take place at national and international levels. We are not just a Church on our own, we need to recognise what other Churches say. We may not be totally bound by it but we need to hear it.

This inevitably raises questions about how the community of faith uses and interprets Scripture and relates the texts of Scripture to the world of today:

The changes we are facing in all sorts of spheres of life, like cloning, like *in vitro* fertilisation, these are not problems that the Bible period had to face. We are being faced with matters of life and death and gender and sexuality, of the way we run our lives and the way we run our ecology. We are faced with questions which are quite unknown to the people who wrote the Bible. If you pick up the book of Leviticus, you'll find there many moral instructions given to the people of Israel, at their time in their history, which are totally inappropriate to us. We don't think stoning people today is right, we don't think that menstruation is an uncleanness and a wickedness, we don't think that someone who has lost an arm shouldn't be brought into the congregation of God. We rather think that such a person should be specially brought into the congregation of God! So when you look at the span of the Bible, over three thousand years, it is not surprising there was some moral change there. One of Jesus' greatest sermons was: 'You heard it said of old time, but I say to you . . .' which was an enormous refining of Old Testament ethics. So yes, the Bible is important to us; yes, we need to listen all the time to what it has to say; yes, it will have tremendous authority over what we decide. But it is not an absolute list of imperatives which mean that we have to obey everything that is written there. Women often go to church without their heads covered; it hasn't brought down the wrath of God on us! We don't believe in circumcision as a religious matter; we might decide it is a health matter or something like that. But these were the raging storms of their day. For us they're not, we are into different storms and we have to deal with them.

I am quite clear that the ethical position given by the New Testament was *not* the once for all to meet all future situations. We plainly know it isn't: they couldn't extend life by machines, they couldn't do heart transplants, they couldn't fly . . . I mean it's just such a different world. And what was so exciting about it was that the Church was promised the Holy Spirit who would guide us into truth. So when we come to the ethical questions of today, we have to trust more in the Spirit of God. That will involve us now in studying prayerfully the tradition in which we live and have our being, the Gospels and the New Testament because that is the foundation of our understanding of God and our understanding of Christ.

The Bible has enormous authority over us. It is not absolute, each line is not absolute. We have to make up our own minds under the guidance of God and in prayer, we have to make up our own minds as to where God wants us to be now.

Knowing that much of Bishop Jim's ministry is spent visiting schools, listening to the views of young people and attempting to engage with the questions they are living with, we asked him to say something about the Church's work with young people. Not surprisingly, he notes that they are intrigued by religious issues but fairly switched off by institutional religion.

There always comes a time when I am talking to sixth-formers when someone says: 'Don't you think the Church is all very boring and irrelevant? What could you possibly say that would persuade me to go to church?' And during my years I've tried to think of many answers to this. Of course, there is a sense in which the worship in which we indulge and which we enjoy and which means a lot to us, can seem very boring to someone who hasn't been through the 250 stages you need in order to get to where worship is meaningful. And yet I have also heard young people say: 'I love the silence . . . I love the sense of mystery.' It is very important not to stereotype all young people. What they feel at the moment is a huge credibility gap. They are quite willing to engage with me and with others about the issues they care about, but they cannot cross over this bridge to being part of the Church. I think we have to cross over a bridge to be part of them and this means really going to them in their situation, understanding what they are at, not nagging. It's rather like being a parent, you have to stay with them and you have to talk with them rationally and not heap them up with your own particular prejudices or strong opinions. You have to give them the space to think, the space to respond.

So what do we do? We really get to know their situation, get to know where they are at and not cut them off before they have had a chance to say what they think. We find routes to be with them on their ground as well as on our ground. I sometimes think that the churches and the parish churches, when they are asked what they can do for young people, say immediately: 'Well, they must come to church, they ought to come to church, they ought to be part of the church.' But I think there is often a lot of prior work to be done. It's lovely when you have a youngster who really loves church and sees the point and that makes you wonder why all the others don't because this person has seen it. I sometimes also say to them: 'Well, the fact of the matter is, you are not taking your soul seriously, but in the end it's up to you to decide whether you think your soul, your personality with God, your relationship with God, is important to you or not. If it is not important to you, then you probably won't come to church and you would certainly be bored if you did.' But if they have inside them something which is saying, 'Well, actually I am quite interested in God; I am quite interested in these things; I would like to explore them', then our job, I think, is to be willing to rush across the bridge, help them explore so that they begin to trust who we are. We take a lot for granted and I don't believe the solution for all young people is great rave services and happy-clappy. That can be important; I have seen great gatherings of young people who are enjoying that, I am not denying it, but it isn't only that. What about those people who are really questioning matters of faith and want to think it through for themselves and really want to work at it? For them, the happy-clappy thing would be a disaster.

So you have to have a varied approach. There will be some who will enjoy monitoring screens, television, films and guitars; there will be people who will respond to this approach and that's important and valuable. But there's a whole raft of young people who think that's really naff and who actually want to work out how Almighty God could allow so much suffering and evil in the world; who want to work out why they shouldn't sleep with their boyfriend or why they should; who want to work out why it is that their friend's just taken an overdose; why it is that the Church seems to present them all the time with sin and doesn't seem to recognise the joys and the hopes of their lives. So what am I talking about? Real engagement. Not everybody is good at it. It doesn't mean that you have to be young. Some of the best friends teenagers have are their grannies and grandpas. But be the person you are with them, exposed to their ways, to their understandings, get on board as you can, whatever age you are, and share their excitements, their passions and their experience.

Finally we asked Bishop Jim to point to some key passages of Scripture that for him particularly reflect the theme of hope:

The Old Testament is full of hope . . . you think of Jacob's encounter in his dream with the angels ascending and descending on the ladder to heaven (Genesis 28:10–19). He is in despair, he is lying in the wilderness, he knows he's done something very wrong. He goes to sleep and there's this wonderful message from God that ultimately God rules and that is a sort of heavenly hope in the face of our wickedness. And of course the wonderful Old Testament hope of Isaiah (chapter 14), the hope of Israel that they will be restored . . . that there will be a highway through the desert, that God will be with them – I mean it's wonderful stuff – 'they will rise up like eagles, they will run and not be weary' . . . the most wonderful declaration of hope.

Then we come to the New Testament. The hope is in the Gospels but hardly mentioned and it all comes alive in the Epistles. It's quite remarkable. Hope bursts out, particularly in St Paul who called God 'the God of Hope' (Romans 15:12–13). But above all, I would say Romans 8:18–39 is a wonderful statement of hope. In fact, that hope is indestructible in the end because it rests in the love of God in Christ Jesus; how hope springs out of frustration in creation, out of the sufferings we have and that we can't be separated from this hope – to me that's wonderful. As for the most powerful image of hope in the Bible, and this is not a conventional answer, but to me it's where I am, one of the greatest signs of hope is Jesus coming into the Garden of Gethsemane and throwing himself headlong and weeping and saying, 'My heart is ready to break with grief'. To me, this is God and therefore I can conceive of no situation in which hope would be dead.

Suggestions for Further Reading
By Bishop Jim Thompson:
Stepney Calling (Mowbray, 1991)
Why God? Thinking Through Faith (Mowbray, 1997)

GROUP WORK

Reminder: These are suggested questions. Please feel free to be selective, adapt them or make up some of your own.

1. 'The earth is charged with the grandeur of God', wrote Gerard Manley Hopkins. Is this a vision that is given to only a few? Why is it not self-evident to all?
2. Why does it make more sense to talk about the mystery of suffering rather than the problem of suffering?
3. 'I do think that hope now is the important thing . . . Of course it involves the future' (p. 68). If you had a different vision of your future, how might it affect the changes you would make in your life now?

4. How does worship help or hinder your perspective of the future?

5. What kind of hope can we talk about with people who have life-threatening diseases, without it sounding like producing 'Christ . . . as some sort of magic rabbit out of the hat'? (pp. 70) What kind of healing ministry is offered in your church? Is it treated as something special or as a natural part of the community's life?

6. We're inclined to think that those who are poor have nothing to give or offer (pp. 71–2). Who are the 'poor' in your community and how could they be said to transfigure it?

7. What are the implications for a society in which there is high unemployment? Why should the Church be involved in unemployment issues? (p. 73) If it isn't, suggest some practical steps that could be taken to put this higher on the agenda.

8. What is the difference between aloneness and loneliness? What are some of the needs of the lonely? How could they be better met through your church?

9. 'I think we have to be much more where people are rather than expect them to come where we are. We are a Church that sees our task as bringing people to Church' (p. 74). How do we set about the task of immersing ourselves deeper in the lives of people where they are? What does this say about the Church's understanding of its mission?

10. In your experience, why have Christians found it difficult to discuss sexual issues? What are we doing about informing ourselves in sexual matters so that we can have a more honest debate in an

atmosphere of mutual trust? How might we hold together our differences when we fail to agree?

11. The Christian community has the task of guarding Scripture. What help is given in your church to understanding the nature of scriptural writings? What more could be done to enable people to have a better understanding of how to interpret Scripture?

12. What are some of the ethical issues we face today that were quite unknown to the people who wrote the Bible? Where can we look for authoritative guidance on these matters?

13. What opportunities present themselves for what Bishop Jim calls 'real engagement' with young people? (p. 80) How could you 'get on board' with them? What does your church need to change in order to be more open and welcoming for young people?

Encountering Scripture
Choose either A or B.

A. Read Romans 8:18–39 slowly and prayerfully.

After a time of quiet reflection, consider what the Spirit might be saying to us through this text and how it could affect our attitude and response to the world around us.

B. You should allow about fifteen minutes for this exercise.
Using the Imagination
In the following exercise, the group can use a passage of Scripture as a way of entering more deeply into its meaning.

One member should be asked to read the passage and 'guide' the group through the questions that follow.

You might like to light a candle in the centre of the group to provide a focus and as a reminder of the presence of Christ 'where two or three are gathered'.

Begin by spending a short period of time becoming still and relaxed. Concentrate on your breathing – allowing each breath to take you deeper. If any worries or concerns arise, simply bring them before God and ask for his help and guidance as you hear the passage.

A group member reads slowly Luke 22:39–45.

After a time of quiet, the following should be read, allowing for a time for reflection between questions.

Picture the scene in your mind, as though you are there as one of the disciples. What do you see?

Picture the garden. What is it like? What are its sounds and perfumes?

• Where is Jesus? What is he doing?
• Picture the other disciples. What are they feeling? How do you feel?
• Begin to use the picture in your mind to form a prayer – or simply remain with God in the silence.
• Let any faces or names come to mind of those you know who are in any kind of distress.
• What might God be saying to you through the experience of your prayer?
• Stay for a moment, quietly reflecting on what God was showing you.

At the end, you might like to share with each other what you wish to.

This prayer can be used at the end of your session.

In gratitude and praise we offer ourselves
with all that we are and have
to God who has given us life.
We offer ourselves to be the bearers of good news
to let people know that God is with them
to let our words be words of love that lead to action
so that men and women may find new hope in
    themselves and each other
for Jesus Christ's sake. Amen.

Session 5

The Home Round the Window

Becoming communities that deeply care through transforming love

with Dame Cicely Saunders

Tree-lined south London suburbs on warm early summer mornings are very pleasant places. After parking our car in a side road not far from St Christopher's Hospice in Sydenham, we walked the few hundred yards to the main building. It is set in an ordinary sort of area, residential, well kept, lots of commuter cars parked alongside big, old houses.

Neither of us was really sure what to expect of St Christopher's Hospice. Perhaps a rambling old house like a nursing home, or maybe a type of cottage hospital. As we walked, the nervousness grew, not simply because we were about to meet someone who is regarded as a well-known figure in the world but also because we were about to walk into a place where people come to be cared for when they are terminally ill.

It's an extraordinary fact that in the course of the last hundred years society has dramatically reversed its attitude to death. In Victorian times, when infant mortality was so rampant, the average family could expect to experience some, if not several, deaths in a short space of time. Such was the abundance of death that grieving, although personal, was not private. In fact, unlike previous generations, the Victorians made it into an industry. Hair bracelets, ornate tombstones, decorated coffins, undertakers' parlours all became the accepted norm to the emerging middle and upper classes. In turn, the public marking of a death became a status symbol and, of course, especially to those who could most afford it.

Today, infant death in Britain, especially of more than one young child in a family, is relatively rare. The life expectancy of adults is so much longer than in 1900. The advance in medical science over the century has been astounding, as has the cost. Our ordinary lives have changed so much that we no longer perceive ourselves to live in the midst of death as our predecessors did. We in the West live in comparative immortality, or so we imagine. Therefore, when death does track us down, it can cause us problems.

Our nation has witnessed one of the most horrific periods for the world, in terms of the destructive forces of war. Britain, amongst many other countries, has experienced the irony of improving health care alongside mass premature death through conflict. Maybe this is something to do with our change in attitude.

The result for many people in postwar generations is that grieving has become not only personal but private. It can be unfamiliar, strange and unexpected. One of us recounted that a friend once said an acquaintance who had not heard of his wife's death called him on the phone. 'How's your wife?' he asked innocently. Knowing that this was not going to be easy our friend hesitatingly replied, 'I'm afraid she died a month ago'. The acquaintance said 'Oh' and put the phone down. It wasn't so much the shock that upset the grieving husband it was the fact that the acquaintance never got back in touch. The shock was understandable but the breakdown in the relationship was painful. Death, to some, is a taboo. They will cross the road in order to avoid a bereaved person and the ongoing healing of the community will be lost.

This is one of the challenges facing churches today. How can we care for the dying and grieving when we are living in and are influenced by this culture which tries to bury the dying before their death? How can we make sense for ourselves of the threshold we call death? How, practically, can we minister to those who hide their grief away? As we entered the friendly, modern and comfortable reception we looked for signs as to how we might address these challenges and three 'moments' helped us see anew.

As we arrived, there was an immediate atmosphere of warmth and professionalism in the reception. The word *clinical* seems to have become associated with a cold form of care that is impersonal and disembodied. Far from it here. Neither was there a bureaucratic kind of management. People were waiting and chatting, others coming and going, some sitting quietly thinking, some striding out purposefully. Why was each of them here? Who might be coming to visit their friend or relative? Who, like us, had come on business? Who might be working and playing their part in this fascinating community? This was a warm, caring and ordinary place.

Then we met Dame Cicely herself, a remarkable woman. Listening to her extraordinary vision and courage to think freely and care so thoroughly for humankind was truly remarkable. The third 'moment' was a throwaway comment at the end of our interview. As we left she said, 'You know your way out, don't you? – Down the stairs, but not too far or you'll end up in the mortuary!' Did we see a wry smile? We weren't sure. But here, this professional community, deeply serious about its work and yet not without wit and fun, empowered by a vision and willing to incarnate victory over death, was ordinary and extraordinary at the same time.

We began by enquiring about how the hospice movement had started and the vision for it all. She told us,

Well, it began with one patient. I was invalided

from nursing and I turned into a medical social worker. In the first ward I took over in St Thomas's there was a Polish Jew of forty who had an inoperable cancer. I followed him up in Outpatients and when he was admitted to another hospital I visited him about twenty-five times in the two months that he was dying. We really became very fond of each other. Before he died he made his will and talking about it he said, 'I'll be a window in your home.'

And so he gave us a commitment to open this hospice to the world, to patients and families, to each other, to beyond, and to be open to all challenges. On another occasion he said, 'I only want what is in your mind and in your heart.' That was a very personal exchange but thinking about it afterwards he meant us to use our minds, all the scientific rigour, all the research, all the learning that could be done but always with the friendship of the heart. After he died, having made his peace with the God of his fathers, – he was an agnostic when I met him – I was at a prayer meeting for All Souls and we started to sing 'How sweet the name of Jesus sounds'. I thought to myself, 'But it didn't to him' and I was absolutely tapped on the shoulder and told, 'He knows me much better than you do already.' I knew that he had made his own journey and thinking about it I thought, 'Yes – in the freedom of the spirit'.

So those are the three founding aims of Hospice:

Openness,   mind together with heart,   freedom of the spirit.

That's how it all started. He died in February 1948 and it took me nineteen years to build the home round the window.

Pastoral care is not an easy term to define. The church needs to work hard in deciding how to reach out to the communities which surround us. So often there is a genuine desire to form pastoral leaders, a visiting team or healing group, but without proper care and attention to how it's going to work, what it's going to attempt and what skills are needed, it can prove to be not only disappointing but also dangerous. Of the three founding aims, the second one, mind and heart together, is the key to ensuring success in this sort of venture. In Dame Cicely's work it is essential to provide good medical science alongside humanitarian care based on beliefs. She told us:

People tend to say they don't go together but they do. I remember taking someone from America around the hospice at least twenty years ago, and he said, 'You have a very sophisticated attitude to medicine, you have a very sophisticated attitude to spirituality or religion and this place feels very comforting and homely, and none of those three ought to go together' – but they do. We are not perfect and it is very important that a hospice is not seen as elitist. In no way must it fail to recognise the good care that is being given by people who don't say, 'I am doing hospice work', 'I am doing palliative care' (which is the more usual professional phrase these days). But we don't say, as it were, to other people, 'I am holier than thou', because we're not. We are very lucky in that we have planned for time. We have time to talk with people. We don't have forty patients in a Cancer Clinic in the morning. How can you give them time? In a hospice where you may do only two or three admissions in a day, you give the patient and the family a feeling of worth. Something is going to be done. There is still hope of some kind or another.

Valuing individuals is one of the modern problems experienced not only by clinics in large hospitals. Churches, like other institutions, sometimes have to face the criticism that they can be impersonal, treating people as if they were all uniform. Dame Cicely several times used the phrase *community of the unlike* to describe the hospice. We asked her to describe what that phrase meant and how it came about.

Well, we started meeting five years before we actually opened – we hadn't even got the land when we started meeting as a group. The then Bishop of Stepney, Evered Lunt, a wonderful pastoral person, was my spiritual director. In the planning, I realised there was a group of people who all knew me but who didn't know each other and they didn't know the Bishop, so we started meeting for a whole day. St Thomas's Hospital lent us a room, and we did that three or four times a year for the five years. I just asked the people who were really interested. I suppose the first day we had twenty or twenty-five, something like that. Looking round the room one realised there was a good atheist in our midst, we were a very mixed group and thinking about it afterwards over the years, I have realised that from the very start we were going to be something of a community with a very small 'c' rather than just a group of professional people doing a job. We were going to be very unlike so we were going to be a community of the *unlike*, as compared with the community I had worked with, the Irish Sisters of Charity, who had a very strong community likeness, although they are very individual as well. We were going to be much more different than ever they were, but we had a commitment to doing the best possible thing for the patient and the family, so we had that in common but pretty well nothing else.

As far as I'm concerned, I had said to God about three years before, 'What do you want me to do?' and I wasn't told until I met David Tasma, this Polish Jew who thought he'd made no difference in the world by having lived in it. He was the one who showed me what I had to do. I had to train as a doctor, and I did endless networking and I listened to thousands of patients. However, all the time I was balancing this with the spiritual foundation which gradually had to open up. I was Church of England. I was rather evangelical – it had to broaden – I was working with Irish Roman Catholic nuns – pre-Vatican II!

But then there was the scientific side. I wouldn't have become a doctor if the surgeon I was working for hadn't said, 'Go and read medicine, it's the doctors who desert the dying, and there's so much more to be learnt about pain. You'll only be frustrated if you don't do it properly and they won't listen to you.' Of course he was right and now there is a whole hospice movement around the world, with its scientific foundations, with its spiritual foundations, Buddhist hospices and secular hospices.

The World Health Organisation's definition of palliative care, as it has come to be called, is relief from the total pain I witnessed: physical, psychological, social and spiritual. The search for meaning is built into the hospice movement. It may be interpreted by people who come from a very secular background, but it comes originally from the Judaeo-Christian ethic and belief.

Hope lies at the very heart of the Judaeo-Christian belief, and in Christianity it is chiefly demonstrated through Jesus dying on the cross. Yet sometimes we use expressions about those near to death like 'I'm afraid it's becoming hopeless' or 'He's a hopeless case'. Could it be that somehow in death hope is lost? For a person who has worked in and around death for many years, Dame Cicely sees hope in many areas of her work:

Oh, I see it in the ordinary people and how they battle through adversity. When we had our thirtieth anniversary in Southwark Cathedral in July we had a group of people who came up with a candle for each of those thirty years – from the day centre, from home-care, from the auxiliaries, from the domestics, from bereavement counsellors and nurses and doctors of course. It was a group of people who would say, 'We've got clay feet just like everyone else'. But they were all making an affirmation that here is something that is enduring, that is changing and developing all the time. I think that everything that grows out of what community we have left in this country and everything that starts to build new community is a signal of hope.

Also, I see hope in the endless learning and finding new things, new people. When we opened,

I remember looking round and thinking everything we have is a gift because we had to raise all the money, it was all given to us. Then some time afterwards I remember, I was giving a talk in chapel, and I suddenly realised I had to say everybody who comes here is a gift, and it may be somebody who comes with a criticism, it may be somebody who comes with a grumble, but that is somewhere where you are going to learn. We have developed a tremendous teaching programme – we are endlessly teaching the people who come here. We have just recently appointed a professor of palliative care between us and a local teaching hospital, King's College. We are tied to the University of London. There is a course going on this week and people – I haven't counted up quite how many countries they are from – will be here for a whole week, thirty of them, learning and showing us new things. One of them comes from Belarus, a children's hospice, a home-care team with children from the Chernobyl fall-out. I met her when I was in Belarus just for a day last year and there's a symbol of hope in the midst of a really terribly difficult situation, in a very poor country with a very strange history. So there is plenty of hope but I think it comes out of a feeling of constant learning, of constant new experiences. Every new patient comes in with their terribly difficult problems, some of them with disastrous situations, I mean that is why they come to a hospice. One has a hope and an expectation that somehow some will be solved. There are some patients about whom we feel well, it wasn't perfect, but we hope it was good enough.

With this in mind we went on to ask Dame Cicely what were her hopes for the future for the hospice movement.

Well, it's against all reason that just one patient should have left £500 and started up what has turned out to be a worldwide movement so I have confidence that as long as we keep listening to our patients we shall know what we have to do. We shall be running *with* the grain of what is needed and the people who are setting out as a children's hospice in Belarus, as hospices in Japan where there is a very *un*religious climate, for people who are battling out into the home in India and Zimbabwe and so on will all, in their different ways, be making their discoveries. I think what is so exciting about the hospice movement is again the community of the *un*like. But as I have said before, it is also a likeness as well. I've just being doing the last bit of an international conference which had 2,000 people from fifty-two different countries. We are all in different cultures, we all have different resources, we all have family values though they may be interpreted rather differently. Yet we have something in common and it is really very exciting to see how this is a growth from a very small seed in each individual country with people of good will and persistence and a very considerable astuteness in how to handle their own individual Health Service. Professor Kastenbaum and I have just edited a book on 'Hospice on the International Scene' with twenty-one chapters on how people started out and where they are now. So I have lots of confidence that this is a mixture of good hard clinical science with a human face which a lot of the world needs.

The hospice movement has now been introduced to many countries and has in some measure begun to dispel the taboo of death. Communities like St Christopher's face up to the reality and inevitability of death and offer care which is well founded in both medical science and social skill. However, unlike disease, there is no cure for death. It is a reality that we have to live with. What can be alleviated is some of the suffering that accompanies it. So we asked Dame Cicely about how we cope with suffering and how we can help others to come to terms with it.

Suffering is a mystery. I think it is a mystery that a God of love actually allows a world in which suffering happens, even if you are quite sure he doesn't specifically send it. But the God whom Christians have been given to believe in is a God who himself suffered and who travels this way with all his children. Let's say someone is suffering, and is saying, 'How could God let my child die?' Harold Kushner who wrote *When Bad Things Happen to Good People* is helpful. Now he hasn't got the vision of God suffering in Christ, but he has got a vision of God suffering alongside, so there is a Jewish view – being able to see it is God sharing that is the answer to the mystery. But even so, if you feel this in your head when you are alongside somebody who is in really desperate need, with a life that has battered them one way or another and is leaving a thoroughly confused and dysfunctional family, even as a Christian I think you still come away saying, 'But God, how could you let this happen?' I think that a faith that never asks questions hasn't got very firm feet on the ground.

In terms of helping others to come to terms with their suffering, I don't think you can ever tell somebody else how to find meaning. I think all you have to do is to search for your own meaning and to go on searching all your life for new meanings, and depth of meanings, some new fresh thing which keeps coming. And if you do that, I think you may perhaps create a climate in which people can make their own search because they have to find their own meaning or maybe they have to stay with feeling, 'I simply don't see meaning here but somehow I will not opt out.' But it's practical as well: doing something for somebody else. I think that the best way to find a meaning in your life is to try and offer something to somebody else. Nobody has nothing to offer and I think that perhaps the most difficult thing to face is the feeling that you have nothing. If you start doing it, if you cross the road instead of going away from the side of somebody whose child has died, you may have no words to say and probably it is much better that you don't and even if your eyes fill with tears, that in itself can be a help. So in an ordinary church – and which church is ordinary anyway! – in a congregation, I don't think we have to look very far to see a job to do.

When it comes to dying, the way that care is given can reach the most hidden places and it may be quite without words. I think people facing the end of a persistent illness may be very lacking in self worth – 'I am only a failure, I didn't respond to treatment.' They've had the battering of operations, of chemotherapy if you're thinking of cancer patients, of a slow deteriorating illness maybe like Parkinson's and so on, and I think people think, 'I am only a burden and perhaps . . .', if we have the pressure for euthanasia, ' . . . I ought to opt out'. I think euthanasia is a terribly dangerous thing. But if we can say as we meet them, either in their own homes or coming in as an in-patient, 'You matter because you are you, and you are good to meet at this moment.' And we go on to say, 'You matter to the last moment of your life and we will do all we can, not only to help you to die peacefully, but to live until you die and that may be not only better but much longer than you expect.' Love is stronger than death, not just *as* strong as death.

I loved David, the Polish Jew I told you about earlier and I loved another Polish man who died after we had a very intense time while he was dying. And I know that love doesn't depend on physical ability, love depends much more on the spirit within a person and that in its turn, to me, depends on the Spirit of God – fruit of the Spirit, love, joy, peace and so on. But you can have love when there isn't peace, when you are parting, and when you are bereaved and I've always found, and I've talked with patients and staff about it in the past, that what really stands at the end of a life is relationships. I've seen far too many people coming to the end of their lives with the feeling that they are going into the next part of the journey which is not they are just snuffed out. I've also seen so many people where the spirit has become stronger as the body has become weaker and I believe that there is something that goes on. It may not be something that you can picture, but there can only be pictures. It's something much stronger than parting.

Finally we talked of images of hope that Dame Cicely finds in Scripture.

Because I have worked among people who were dying for so many years, I go to Revelation 21. The city has four walls and three gates in each wall so wherever you start to go towards it you find an open gate waiting for you. I think it's an image which says to us, 'Wherever you are, whatever you are like, whatever you believe, you are going to find a welcome'. To me that is a wonderful image of hope and the river through the city and the leaves of the tree for the healing of the nations are a very vivid picture of all the things that one longs for. I see a young mother, divorced maybe, leaving children and wondering who is going to care. 'Who is going to love my children?' It's a most poignant last word and it is very difficult to see hope in that situation. But one of our atheists, and we have them here, found herself saying in a meeting the other day, 'All shall be well', which, of course, is an echo of Julian of Norwich. I think that the idea that there is a welcome from wherever you come from is my favourite picture.

I love Julian of Norwich. When I 'met her' I gradually learned that here she was in Norwich, fourteenth century, Hundred Years' War, Black Death, Peasants' Revolt, all the awful things that were happening and yet she was full of joy, full of hope but also tremendously concerned for her fellow Christians. It wasn't just an individual vision, she was sure it was for everybody. It was her vision of Christ's suffering but yet his joy and triumph within the cross and I just found the way she wrote inspirational.

She's always, as it were, looking at a jewel from another facet. I found in reading her, as I have done in the mornings over the years, there is always something new. This morning I was reading 'The Lord and the Servant' and her comments on that particular showing where she sees Adam representing all men falling into a ditch getting into terrible trouble, but there was no wrath in God. I found that enormously good. Oh yes, I know, as she sees the servant running from his lord and getting into terrible trouble, she identifies the servant with Christ also. That's why God has no wrath in him because he always sees us in Christ, all those who shall be saved. I personally believe along with John Austin Baker that when Christ became man, God brought all men in as his children, not just the ones who made a profession of faith.

So Julian is somebody who is an enormously optimistic yet very realistic person. She certainly saw hope in the crucifix and the showing that she had of the blood. She describes it in a very fourteenth-century way and we can't see the cross or the crucifix without the resurrection behind it. It's the cross itself which is the victory and Easter Day is the seal of what has already happened.

As to other passages of Scripture, well there is one that I would immediately turn to – Romans 5: 'More than that we rejoice in our sufferings, knowing that the suffering produces endurance and endurance produces character and character produces hope and hope does not disappoint us because God's love has been poured into our hearts through the Holy Spirit.' I mean what can we ask more than that?

Someone has said that we don't really begin to live until we have come to terms with death. What the hospice movement is doing is helping us to become familiar with this great unknown through which we look to glimpse eternity. Dame Cicely describes the hospice movement as a home round a window, a fascinating image of the familiarity of our home and the exploration of looking through the window to the beyond.

All this is part of a greater movement which is paying attention to the way things die and are resurrected. Wider than personal mortality, we are struggling with the end of marriages, the end of older employment patterns, the decline in popularity and influence of institutions like the Church, the legal system and the monarchy. As we might hear at a funeral service, 'In the midst of life we are in death', death is everyday and we are called to pray for resurrection. Instead of throwing things away, we recycle. Instead of pulling down old buildings we redevelop them for new initiatives. Instead of allowing faith to decline in the postmodern world, we are reshaping it, redefining it, restating it in new worship, new collaborative leadership, new ways of being Church.

The Christian hope, which we found in St Christopher's, shines forward to illuminate a path into, through and beyond death. But it also reflects back into this life a responsibility which influences how we live today. Are we living our lives with the knowledge that one day we shall die? The hospice movement challenges the Church to be open to hope in what can often be a cynical world, to work hard with both mind and heart, to be courageous and to think and speak freely. The Church needs to be a home for those who feel hopeless, and for those who already feel it is home, a window to look into another world.

Suggestion for Further Reading
Cicely Saunders (ed.), *Beyond the Horizon: A Search for Meaning in Suffering* (DLT, 1990)

GROUP WORK

Reminder: These are suggested questions. Please feel free to be selective, adapt them or make up some of your own.

1. It's said that the Victorians 'made death into an industry'. What are the ways that our contemporary society manages death?

2. How have our attitudes to dying and death changed since Victorian times? Could it be said that we have a healthier attitude today?

3. What are some of the issues in the local community which you believe could be helped through your church's pastoral care? What hinders or helps you in being more effective?

4. Dame Cicely talks about the hospice having time to care for patients (pp. 93–4) In what ways does your church community give time to give care where it is needed? How does it prioritise its time and energy? Are there other priorities that also need more attention? If so, which ones?

5. How do you resist the temptation of becoming a community of like-minded people? What would it mean to 'have the mind of Christ' in a community of the unlike? (pp. 94–5)

6. What does your church do in giving support to those who are dying and their loved ones? What resources do you draw upon?

7. What issues are around for you over the question of euthanasia? Can you think of situations when euthanasia might be the right of an individual to make a free choice? Are there any circumstances in which you would wish to make that choice for yourself? What would be the dangers for society?

8. Are there any experiences of dying that members of the group could share? What was it that contributed to the dying being either a positive or a negative experience? What can we learn from this?

9. 'Wherever you are, whatever you are like, whatever you believe, you are going to find a welcome' (p. 102). Do you agree with Dame Cicely in this? What would stand in the way of this sentiment being misunderstood? You might like to read what she also has to say on page 103 in talking about Julian of Norwich's 'The Lord and the Servant'.

10. Dame Cicely speaks of the 'leaves of the tree for the healing of the nations' (p. 102). Discuss some of the ways you believe your church contributes to wider healing and reconciliation in society.

11. 'In the midst of life we are in death'. What are some of the things that ought to die in the institutional Church so that there might be a true resurrection? Why are we more fascinated about survival than death?

12. The symbol of a home round a window is a very

powerful image. It is both strange and familiar, for we don't generally have windows inside houses, they are meant for us to look out on the world. But what if the window was positioned so that we could look at another dimension, to look beyond our everyday lives to a hope beyond?

Jesus said the kingdom is within. In what ways might the window be leading to a better vision of God's realm?

Could death be in fact a window within the world to help see eternity and, once opened, for us to experience it?

Our everyday lives often go by without a second thought. Maybe the window speaks to us of looking more carefully at the ordinary things in the midst of life.

Take some time in the group to contemplate, in silence, this paradoxical image.

Afterwards, allow the group time to share feelings, thoughts and reflections.

Encountering Scripture

The group should sit comfortably with eyes closed while a member reads slowly Revelation 21:1–6.

Members should try and picture the kind of 'new day' that they would like to see happen. They should let different images come to the surface. What do they see? What do they hear? How do they feel them?

Allow about 4–5 minutes for quiet reflection. Then ask the group to jot down some of the images to share later.

Then, again with eyes closed, ask the following questions to reflect on. What kind of church would you like to become in the next five years or so? What kind of people do you see belonging to this church?

What do you see them doing?

Again allow 4–5 minutes to jot down a few ideas, then end this exercise by letting members reflect on and share their thoughts. Are there differences and similarities? Are there any implications? If so, who might this information be shared with next?

You may like to conclude this session with the following prayer:

> O spring in the desert
> O shelter from the heat
> O light in the darkness
> O guide for the feet
> O joy in the sadness
> O support for the weak
> O Lord with us always
> Your Presence we seek
>
> ('Desert Waters' by David Adam)

Appendix: Notes for Group Leaders

1 Before the Group Meets

Think about your group. What kind of people come to it?
What sort of issues do they/might they like to discuss? How
much help do they need to get going? Will you need to
make a summary of the chapter as an introduction or will
they be happy to get going straight away? How can you
match the material in the book and tape to your group
members?

How much time will you allocate for each session? Will
you need time for things other than the session itself –
coffee, prayer, sharing news, arranging the next leader/venue
etc.? If you want to finish on time, take these things into
account.

Are there any individuals in the group who might not be
able to read or anyone who has difficulties in learning? How
will you help them?

How will you arrange the room? Think about the position
of the chairs and their comfort. Remember that some people
like a hard chair. Consider the lighting: too low and
people become irritated. Warmth: too little – the brain
seizes up; too much – the people go to sleep!

You may like to include the group members and the Lent
Course in your intercessions.

2 Preparation

Listen to the tape and read the session in the book. Try to take some time to think about what the contributor is saying. Jot down a few thoughts about the session that might interest the group.

Read the questions set at the end of the session. We have provided more than you will need so that you and the group can be selective. Pick out three or four that might interest the group or let them spur you on to make up some of your own. Remember that our questions can be adapted.

Check that your questions are open ones – that they are not going to be answered by a simple yes or no, as in a closed question. So use when, why, how, etc.

Are you going to ask the group members to do anything before the group meets? For example, to underline the most interesting part of the session in the book or even listen to the tape.

If you are not using the tape you will need to work out an order for the questions you are going to use. Try to begin where people are. We all find it easier to say something when it's about our own experience. You may want to begin with an 'icebreaker' such as 'Tell the group one thing you enjoyed about church this week' or 'What issues have been around for you since the last session?'

People appear to learn best when they learn together, which is one of the reasons these Lent groups work. You may find that you get to the end of a session without any definite conclusions but that people have learned a great deal through the discussion.

Check your timing. Timing is so important and can even sometimes determine whether a person comes back the following week. Remember that the tape, if you use it, will take about fifteen minutes. The tape is divided into sections with suggestions about which questions apply to what you have heard.

Consider where you might be able to speed up the progress of the group or what you might have to leave out if time is short.

3 Resources

People sometimes find it helpful to write things down, so have some pens and pencils handy just in case someone hasn't brought one. You may want to write up some significant points as you go along. You could use a flip chart but these are expensive and sometimes too large for a small room. How about using a cardboard box covered with the reverse side of wallpaper? It can sit on a small table in the middle of the room and you or others can write on it with a marker.

It may be helpful to have a Bible or two available for those who forget theirs and of course you will need a cassette player for the tape. Also, some groups like to have a symbol to focus on for prayers, for instance, a candle or a picture.

4 At the Meeting

Arrive early to get the room ready. Liaise with the host about when to serve refreshments. Try to begin as soon as possible after the stated start time. Sometimes groups get later and later until eventually they don't meet at all!

At the first meeting, agree on a time to finish and stick to it.

As the discussion is progressing, jot down one or two notes in order to sum up at the end. Encourage everyone to speak but don't force them. Allow time for a reflective quiet; this can be very useful for deeper learning. Be ready to change your outline, depending on interest and time. Have to hand the other questions that you didn't fully prepare, just in case they become relevant. Remember, most leaders fear before the study that they will 'dry up' and afterwards that they had too much material! Especially at the end, allow a moment for people to think about what they have discovered in the study.

You may need to stop people from talking as well as draw others out. If there is someone in the group who talks too much on a regular basis, sit next to him or her, and say, 'Let's hear from others who haven't spoken yet or very much'. Organise it so that all the members of the group in turn have an opportunity to say what they think about an issue (allowing people to 'pass' if they wish). If any individuals persist in dominating the group, you may have to speak to them outside the meeting, on their own.

Some groups like to pray at the beginning, some in the middle, some at the end, some not at all. Some like the leader to say a prayer, some want a corporate prayer like the Lord's Prayer, some want to use silence, some want an extemporary prayer time. Be sensitive. We have suggested a prayer for the group to use at the end of each session.

5 After the Session

Take a little time to think about how it all went and what could be improved for the next time. Experience shows that people feel happier sharing the leadership of a group with someone else. So two heads will be better than one in helping you to do this important reflective work.

With a little preparation the group can really be fun – so enjoy it!